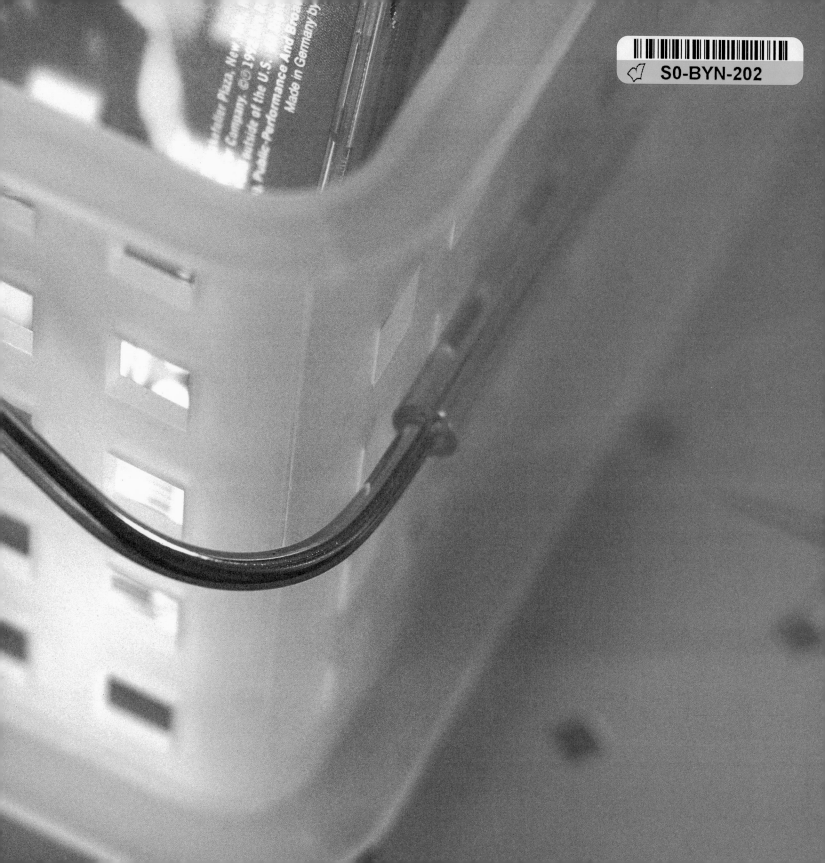

The Storage Book

The Storage Book

Over 250 ideas for stylish home storage

Cynthia Inions

First published by Lyons Press 2000

First published in Great Britain in 1997
by Mitchell Beazley, an imprint of Octopus Publishing Group Limited
2-4 Heron Quays
London E14 4JP

The text of this book was set in Gill Sans.
Printed and bound in China.

First edition
2 4 6 8 10 9 7 5 3 1

ISBN 1-58574-204-X

contents

introduction

below Inexpensive clear and opaque plastic products in plain and simple style offer multiple storage solutions in living areas, garages, and workshops. (Unit from Muji.)

left Reuse industrial or office furniture and fixtures as practical storage items. A clothing locker from a public swimming pool is given new status as a key storage item in a New York studio apartment.

below Modern manufacturers constantly rework traditional storage concepts such as roll-top desks or decorative armoires in keeping with multifunctional homes. (Carlo Madera bureau.)

left An inventive alternative to traditional jars for storing herbs and spices, this is a simple combination of a plastic bag and an airtight clip – keeping its contents fresh. Hang multiple bags in a horizontal line.

above Combine modern, state-of-the-art design with basic practicality in singular storage items like this impressive Stanley cupboard. (Manufactured by Dialogica.)

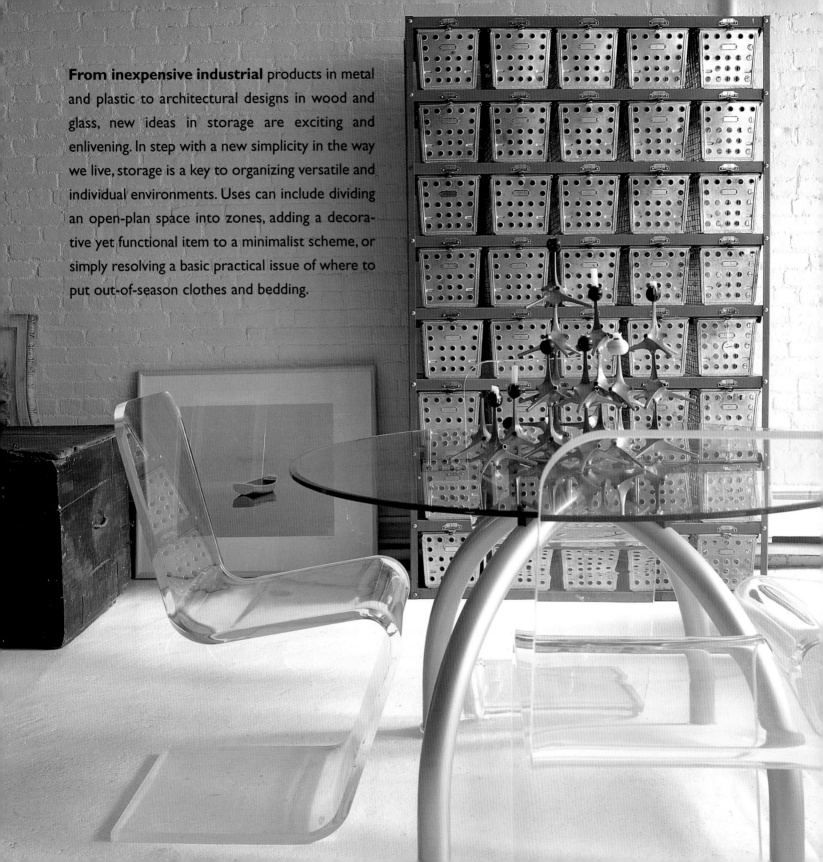

From inexpensive industrial products in metal and plastic to architectural designs in wood and glass, new ideas in storage are exciting and enlivening. In step with a new simplicity in the way we live, storage is a key to organizing versatile and individual environments. Uses can include dividing an open-plan space into zones, adding a decorative yet functional item to a minimalist scheme, or simply resolving a basic practical issue of where to put out-of-season clothes and bedding.

Of the many inspirational and practical storage solutions to revolutionize kitchens, liberate bedrooms, and transform living space, some will meet your current requirements exactly, while others will need a little modification to fit in perfectly.

Some schemes will suggest a whole new way to live. Perhaps it is time to review and reorganize your domestic environment. Yet before investing in new storage or a structural redesign, begin with a critical edit of everything you possess, from kitchen utensils, clothing, books, and electrical equipment to furniture and fixtures and fittings.

Simplicity, freedom, and a sense of space are not about finding a place to store every single thing. They are about identifying what is essential, functional, and inspirational, keeping these elements and giving away, selling, or recycling everything else. Consider efficient industrial shelving when planning kitchens; simplify living space with modular storage cabinets for everything from tableware to CD players and books; or screen all your clothes and bed linen behind translucent sliding glass panels in bedrooms.

Of the many inspirational ideas in this book, the majority can fit into your home with ease to solve difficult storage problems.

above Semi-transparent doors or sliding panels signal an exciting direction in storage design, as seen in this cupboard by Maarten Van Severen.

left A preference for combining kitchen and dining space places a new emphasis on kitchen planning and design. Opt for an efficient easy-to-maintain system with ample hideaway storage to provide a simple but welcoming environment. (Mediterranea by Arc Linea.)

left New designs like this magazine rack offer fresh thinking on conventional storage. For alternative ad hoc solutions, use filing cabinets for clothing or metal trash cans for laundry to add vitality to everyday storage solutions.

right Dynamic sculptural forms such as this, or artistic storage items in wood, glass, or stone add a welcome organic element to minimalist areas.

storage with style

period
style

Grand memorials to a different age, period storage pieces can work within a contemporary interior if you adopt a minimalist approach. Unless you favor living in historically faithful surroundings, cut back or pack away ornaments, simplify decoration with plain colors, and install impressive storage items that have a degree of formality and symmetry – ideally, a single expansive piece for every situation. For example, a good-size armoire can provide ample storage for books, china, foodstuffs, clothing, or electronic equipment in just about any setting. A chest of drawers is equally versatile, while colonial-style chests and wicker hampers will provide extra small-scale storage.

left An antique chest of drawers is the main storage item in the library of a New York conversion. It stands formally at one end of the main room to define a writing and reading space. A packing trunk and ethnic baskets store paperwork. (Design: Tricia Foley.)

above Simple log baskets on each side of an imposing stone and carved-wood mantel fulfill an essential fireside storage function. They also make attractive alternatives to the traditional type of ornamental container. (Design: Tricia Foley.)

left Too precious and formal to use for food, an antique silver platter makes an imaginative flatware storage tray. Decorative and practical, it can be transferred easily from kitchen shelf to any table setting.

Simplicity and freedom from clutter was the defining feature of a Shaker dwelling. Shaker homes were havens of orderliness, in tune with strict spiritual beliefs. For believers, living as large communal families and sharing everything, it was essential that even the smallest household item had a place in which everyone would know where to find it, use it, and put it back for the next person. Mother Ann, founder of the Shakers in North America in the 1770s, set out directives for this orderly way of life. Her guidelines were plain common sense: "Provide places for all your things so that you may know where to find them at any time, day or night."

shaker style

left Peg rails can take on a different use in every room. Thread lengths of rope or leather through shelf tops and loop them over peg rails in kitchens, bathrooms, and halls for small-scale storage.

below These sculptural storage boxes and bowls are as appropriate to a period dwelling as a modern interior. Color-code individual items to identify what is inside.

above Saucepans and shelves for spice jars hang from a peg rail, making them easily accessible for cooking and food preparation. Built-in kitchen cabinets provide a place for everything in a simple arrangement of multisized drawers under an oiled-wood counter.

opposite A peg rail running around a plain wall is a key feature of a Shaker-style interior for storing essential everyday items. Shakers did not believe in display for the sake of it, so if you do not use an item often, do not hang it on a peg rail.

The simplicity and honest functionalism of historic Shaker dwellings, with a delight in space and respect for nature's gifts, is essential inspiration for contemporary interiors. Simple storage along Shaker lines organizes objects according to common sense: each item is given a place appropriate to how often it is used, or to its size and function. Storage furniture can include floor-to-ceiling cabinets and chests of drawers in pine, maple, and cherry wood for storing all kinds of household items from tableware to clothing. Peg rails around every room provide easy-access hanging space for brooms and everyday items, keeping the floor clear and easy to sweep. Freestanding furniture is best kept to a minimum, with only as many chairs as people to sit on them. And when chairs are not in use, store them off the floor on the peg rails. Everything should play a part efficiently and harmoniously — another key Shaker directive that is as relevant now as it was to Mother Ann in the 1770s.

left Shaker ladderback chairs are designed for hanging out of the way on pegs when not in use. Make sure that your peg rail is securely anchored to a wall before you hang any kind of chair in this way.

country
style

above Hanging by a nail on a wall in a utility room, a shallow basket is a useful container for a jumble of pegs and sticks. It exemplifies the practicality of country style.

right A country kitchen flatware tray with a central division neatly frames and separates antique knives and forks for decorative and functional storage.

above Old-fashioned food "safes" with fine wire mesh on wooden frames make useful storage cabinets for china, table linen, and dry food or cans.

right A wooden bucket with individual staves bound in place by a metal hoop is a convenient place to store kitchen utensils and turns everything it contains into a decorative feature.

From pocket-sized cottages to grand houses, or even urban interiors with an identity crisis, the traditions at the heart of country style – mixing, not matching – will apply. This means the freedom to combine inexpensive thrift-store finds, homespun antiques, special pieces that have a family history, and anything you like the look of.

left In this informal New York apartment, decoration is in homespun-style. A ceramic dish overflowing with family photographs and a painted box used to store letters provide personal effects with originality and spirit.

below A French wire basket split into sections provides simple but effective storage for glasses. Stack this type of lightweight container with glasses, bottles of olive oil, and jars of condiments or spices and carry it directly to the table – indoors or out.

right Strong lines on simple furniture are key to the appeal of country-style interiors. This kitchen hutch provides ample storage for all kitchen items, plus additional space to display a collection of antique china.

Adhering to a single period style — or even choosing furniture from one country of origin — will not result in a typically informal country-style mix. To get the look right, start with distinctive basics — for kitchens, perhaps a scrubbed Italian table with a flatware drawer and an English hutch. A less conventional alternative would be to mix an individual shelf unit with a contrasting chest of drawers. For living rooms, look out for European painted food "safes"; these are ideal for storing books and stereo equipment. And decorative Spanish or French armoires provide ample storage in country-style interiors. Visit flea markets and auctions, and consider stripping or painting anything you find there. Keep a set of room measurements with you before you buy.

Once you have decided on your main pieces of country-style storage furniture and installed them, you can add the smaller items: traditional ceramics, decorative metalware, and anything craft-oriented, like handmade boxes. For inexpensive solutions, check out local farmer's markets or supermarkets for vegetable boxes or wooden crates—they are perfect for kitchen storage.

In a radical break with traditions in craft and ornamentation, modernist designs from 1910 to the 1950s were influenced by new technology. The bold architectural shapes of modernist pieces, mass produced from industrial plastics, plywood, and steel, still generate a buzz and exert a powerful influence on contemporary designs. Many originals continue to be produced, so it is possible to buy the real thing. Alternatively, collect classics from dealers or markets, track down inexpensive chain-store equivalents, or take inspiration from the colors and simple shapes of these pieces to revamp existing storage items with metal doors, new pulls, and paint.

contemporary
inspiration

below Highly architectural and colorful, Charles Eames's storage cabinet combines form and function. In a living area, such a piece can provide useful storage for electrical equipment and books.

right In this New York galley kitchen, built-in storage cabinets and appliances are installed along one wall. This creates a space for table and chairs. (Architects: Fernlund + Logan.)

left Inspired by mass-produced designs from the 1950s, this horizontal aluminum wall track system with organic-looking brackets provides an architectural support for heavy-duty glass shelving. (Design: Ali Tayar.)

below The Isoken donkey provides compact multi-storage for living room paraphernalia, including magazines, newspapers, and books, in lightweight sculptural plywood.

right Postwar Scandinavian design brings a modernist perspective to a New York apartment. A teak cabinet stores CDs in an open-plan area. (Architects: Solveig Fernlund & Neil Logan.)

left To modernists, metal in design is the equivalent of concrete in architecture – bold and essential. This revamp to replace wood veneer cabinet doors with inexpensive metal gives an ordinary New York kitchen-in-a-corridor a dynamic new look.

left The graphic boxlike dimensions of a 1950s Knoll teak cabinet with painted steel legs is offset by traditional paneling. The glass vases are modern. For modernist storage on a budget, mount square kitchen wall cabinets on the wall at sideboard height and customize them further with paint or a change of pulls.

Storage cabinets in the spirit of modernism have a utilitarian simplicity. Many contemporary geometric or modular designs encompass this industrial style, from boxlike television cabinets to cubic bookcases. Put together a wall of cubes with interchangeable solid and glass doors and create your own modernist version. Leave some cubes open, with or without shelves. A strong geometric frame will overpower the disorder within, so a typical jumble of books and magazines will not look out of place.

Explore the potential of boxlike wall cabinets. Kitchen suppliers usually stock a good selection. Install a row along a hallway, bedroom, or living room at sideboard height with invisible hardware. Place one cabinet in a bathroom for toiletries, or make a square of four in a living room to store books or videos – perhaps paint them different colors, or experiment with one color for the frame and different colors for each door.

Even if your budget does not run to new designs, it is possible to enjoy the poetic plainness of the modern movement. Paint existing cabinets and change pulls to simple metal disks, or replace doors with metal or plastic panels.

Beyond presenting almost limitless storage possibilities, ethnic furniture and folk artifacts from around the world seem to exert a magical spell on the postindustrial dwellers of the Western world. The bright colors of African baskets or the graphic simplicity of a Japanese chest can add a powerfully primitive or exotic presence to a modern interior. The key to incorporating these elements successfully into modern settings is to put them to use as functional everyday items.

ethnic
ideas

left A simple 19th-century temple cupboard in teak from West Rajasthan, India forms part of a collection in David Wainwright's London town house. Set on wooden wheels, it transfers easily to a modern interior.

left In the spirit of a cave dwelling, this hewn stone and wood nightstand exerts a powerful force in a California interior. Along with kitchen cabinets made out of driftwood-effect planks, wicker baskets, and large pots, storage is primitive style.

above Often lacking in modern interiors, decoration is an essential feature of ethnic art. An elaborate artifact or piece of furniture, like this finely carved Nuristani chest offset by a plain backdrop, can be both practical and decorative.

right Textile designer Jack Lenor Larsen brings Japanese aesthetics to a collection of ceramics, sculpture, and paintings in a New York apartment. Set out with precision on glass shelves within a wooden framework, the collection is seen or hidden, thanks to traditional sliding screens.

Inspirational as well as exotic, many ethnic storage ideas originate from ancient cultures and lifestyles and were designed to be portable – for example, stacking and nesting baskets from space-conscious Japan, wooden merchants' chests from spice-trading India, and woven sacks for clothing and cooking pots from the nomadic shepherds of the Atlas mountains.

Still being made today, and using methods and materials little changed for centuries and easily transportable for travelers and tourists, many bold and simple items transfer well to modern-day interiors as essentially practical storage solutions.

With furniture – particularly wooden items such as a Mexican sideboard or Korean trunk – it is a good idea to buy imports from specialist dealers close to home. There is less risk of an infestation of exotic insects and, unless the item was shipped very recently, less chance of climatic shock reaction – such as splitting or cracking wood.

left A majestic antique Japanese *mizuya*, once a silent witness to formal tea ceremonies, in cypress wood provides flexible storage with an array of drawers and sliding panels.

right Hand-woven baskets on open wooden shelves provide decorative and accessible small-scale storage in a New York bedroom. Like a visual index, the pattern, color, and shape of each basket identifies its contents.

above A wall of cabinets in blue are the main feature of this interior. (Courtesy of the Atlanta Historical Society, Inc.)

left Malcolm Temple's ornamental sea chest is crafted from basic building materials. The frame is carved, stained, and varnished composite board and gives an appearance of Oriental wood.

Specialist dealers in ethnic items can provide essential back-up and advice about cleaning, repair, and restoration. For inexpensive small-scale storage solutions — such as baskets, metalware, wooden bowls, and boxes — check out your local shopping mall, craft stores, and craft fairs.

Selecting ethnic storage pieces that are functional as well as decorative is very important. Presenting a Rajasthani temple cupboard as an artistic souvenir will alienate it from its new surroundings; however, put into useful service as a linen or china chest, its relocation will make sense.

Folk art pieces such as Pueblo Indian water jars or punch-pattern tin boxes from New Mexico can all find new identities as decorative yet essentially practical storage items. Aim to be selective, and think about how ethnic colors and organic shapes will fit in with modern-day industrial precision and exactness. For example, a vast handmade terra-cotta grain jar, bargained for with passion in a Moroccan souk, will invariably look quite different on a concrete floor in an urban kitchen. Yet juxtapositions like this can express the power of ethnic design.

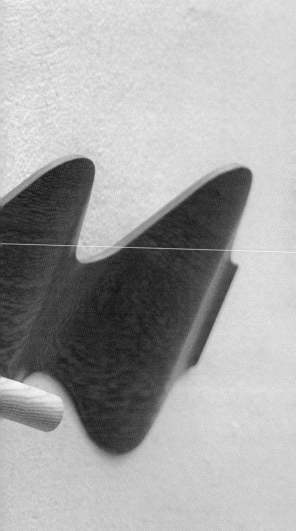

hall and porch

hall and
porch

Entrance halls are active transition areas from outside to inside and require effective storage for dropping off or picking up outdoor clothing, a change of footwear, keys, mail, and perhaps a bicycle. Yet entrance halls should also be welcoming spaces – the first space that you and your visitors will see. So it is important to create a practical, friendly space that is free from clutter or an impassable collection of disorderly clothes or equipment. Ideally, keep the area directly inside the front door clear for quick and easy access, and plan any storage solutions to begin beyond the doormat.

left The area behind this sweeping stairway provides storage for cleaning equipment, tools, and out-of-season household items. (Architects: Munkenbeck + Marshall.)

above A photographer's trunk converted to household storage is in keeping with this industrial-style interior. A collection of antique clocks cleverly inhibits a buildup of clutter.

right An open-plan studio becomes a work/living space with the addition of a bed platform, basic stair, and a partition to create an office. A hat stand defines the entrance area.

For clothing, umbrellas, and bags, there is a wide choice of hooks – from minimalist metal buttons to wooden pegs or decorative iron-work – that will fit in with contemporary or traditional environments. A wooden or metal pole spanning an alcove and equipped with a good supply of coat hangers will provide useful hanging space. If space is available and storage requirements exceed a few coat hooks, line hall walls with cabinets or a combination of shelves and hanging rods. Folding doors, sliding panels, and roll-up shades provide space-conscious alternatives to conventional doors.

Within an open-plan environment, consider constructing a simple enclosure to create storage and a sense of division from inner and outer space. A permanent wall or panel, or a less dense glass partition to let light pass through, will provide an essential cut-off from the front door and offer a potential storage area with hooks attached to the wall or a freestanding coat stand or clothes rod.

left A simple sandblasted glass screen conceals a basic clothes rod and contrasts to great effect with a traditional hall table and collection of artifacts. (Architects: Stickland Coombe.)

Hall landings can present welcome and surprising storage possibilities. A bookshelf placed next to a chair and good light can offer a peaceful reading spot. Alternatively a desk, table, or flip-down worktop with shelves for paperwork and files above can provide office or study space. All kinds of cabinets, from armoires to custom-built designs that make the best use of any odd corners, are perfect for over-spill or out-of-season clothing, linen, spare bedding, books, or sports equipment.

Understair cabinets provide useful storage for bulky items like vacuum cleaners, ironing boards, and the usual closet overspill. If there is space, put in a cupboard or shelf for valuable extra storage. If space is really limited, consider the potential for storage above door-ways. A shelf across the width of a door frame on bracket supports is useful for books. If you want to conceal a jumble of odds and ends, store them in boxes on the shelf. Consider extending the shelf to run around a landing or along a row of doorways. (Check that this will not create an obstruction before you go ahead.) Alternatively, frame a door-way with narrow shelves from floor to ceiling and create a mini-library.

left A traditional wooden peg rail for coats, and bare floorboards for heavy-duty footwear and walking sticks provide highly functional and down-to-earth storage in this basic mudroom in Stephen Mack's house.

above Narrow tables provide ideal storage for busy hallways, and simple structures like this folding plant table take up less space than formal pieces.

left It is hard to beat a peg rail for practical storage in a hall. Perhaps put two peg rails at different heights in the hallway for adult and children's outdoor clothing.

living room

open and shut
cases

Whether you spend time reading, listening to music, watching television, or relaxing on a sofa with friends, flexible storage solutions are the key to organizing a multifunctional and informal living space. From building-block modular cabinets with open and shut storage to architectural holes in the wall, modern ideas for accommodating diverse recreational interests will contribute to creating an environment that is both practical and personal.

above This pearwood table with a glass top includes a drawer underneath for magazines and books, and space for games, collections, and specialized items. (From Arc Linea.)

above This flexible arrangement of storage building blocks features shelves and divisions. Begin with one square and add on new cabinets to meet requirements. (From Arc Linea.)

left A simple wooden "D" shelf with steel brackets can create a striking display for a selection of art books and personal memorabilia. (Design: Annabelle Selldorf.)

right Simplicity, light, and space are key elements in this New York apartment. A simple early 20th-century French cabinet contrasts with a plain shelf for displaying prints. (Design: Vicente Wolf.)

Storing every possession on view can look chaotic and overpower a living space, yet if everything is hidden away, a room can appear unwelcoming. For a sense of order with a human touch, mix open and shut storage for entertainment equipment as well as displays of selected personal items.

Individual preference is a good guide when planning what to reveal and what to conceal — especially if you have one main leisure activity. For multifunctional spaces, select something of all key interests to be displayed and conceal bulky back-up equipment or specialized collections. Alternatively, use specific storage items, perhaps a cabinet or shelf system, for individual activities and divide a living space into recreational zones.

Store collections of videos, CDs, or books in a set of drawers, a cabinet, or a storage system with sliding front panels. Keep a selection of current favorites on hand in an open rack, single shelf, or simple informal stack.

right This spacious living area contains a mixture of open and shut storage. CDs and videos reside in a set of drawers, while African artifacts are displayed on a simple oak table. (Furniture designer/maker: Andrew Mortada.)

Using open storage to display artifacts, collections, photographs, or anything of personal interest that is visually stimulating enlivens any space. Choose a storage system that is relevant to the items that you intend to display. For example, a bold system of parallel wooden shelves is perfect for displaying modern sculpture or black-and-white photographic prints in a contemporary environment, yet it might overpower a colorful collection of American folk art or Japanese ceramics.

Before opting for a particular storage system – either open shelving or shelves within a framework – check the weight and space requirements of the items. If a collection of artifacts or electronic equipment is complete, opt for permanent shelving with wall brackets or metal supports; or, for invisible mountings, embed metal rods into the wall and then into the back of wooden shelves.

Lay out everything for display on the floor and map out an arrangement or make a storage plan. Double-check measurements with special attention to depth, and leave adequate space front and back, especially for equipment with cables and connections.

left An effective contrast of modernity and antiquity in a New York apartment. A display shelf for photographs is an ideal, flexible storage solution. (Design: Vicente Wolf.)

below In keeping with a graphic modern environment, a wall shelf with invisible hardware presents a clean-cut profile. (Furniture from Arc Linea.)

right A collection of cheap and cheerful figures from South America are displayed prominently on this network of glass shelves within a simple wooden framework.

left A strikingly simple wall-mounted shelving system with tracks and adjustable brackets in anodized aluminum is as visually appealing as the ceramics on display. (Ellen's Brackets by Ali Tayar for Parallel Design.)

Some storage options are in fact architectural solutions – structural add-ons or details that appear to be part of the framework of a space. Ambitious ideas, such as replacing partition walls with floor-to-ceiling storage systems accessible from both sides, or adding a parallel wall next to an existing wall to create storage space in between, require forward planning and imagination. For ideas on this scale, consult an architect for creative input and incorporate any suggestions or recommend-ations at the initial planning or refurbishment stage for maximum economy and minimal disruption.

For minimalists, the appeal of structural storage is to devise a practical framework for living free from the clutter of individual items of furniture, while allowing for possessions. However, be aware that this level of simplicity throws into relief anything on display. Keep visible elements either honest and functional, or sculptural and artistic; perhaps a compact music system, African figure, or Japanese light.

right A desk and video shelf, suspended between a sculptural plaster wall and original metal support, links traditional and modern architectural details in a workshop conversion. (Furniture designer/maker: Andrew Mortada.)

right Basic cabinets have been upgraded with gold leaf and varnish. They consist of a stack of two individual cabinets, with TV, video, and music equipment under lock and key, and children's toys below. (Design: Justin Meath Baker.)

below A sculptural music cabinet in beaten lead, aluminum, and wood provides storage for a bank of equipment, and adds a powerful presence in a modern environment. (Weymouth cupboard and CD cabinet by Malcolm Temple.)

Even in high-tech warehouse or loft conversions, on-view entertainment equipment can often look too raw and industrial. In a conventional house or apartment, managing this juxtaposition is a challenge. Yet entertainment equipment is now a key element in many living spaces, so aim to incorporate equipment in an accessible yet stylish way.

Function and decoration can be combined by using distinctive storage items to conceal bulky or incongruous pieces of equipment. Alternatively, customize an existing cabinet. Transform inexpensive composite or pine cabinets with silver or gold leaf and varnish or architectural molding. Use contrasting paint colors or cover them with burlap, string, or thin sheets of zinc or copper; change the existing pulls to cut-glass spheres or something organic like twigs or found driftwood. For modern eclectics, eccentric gothic-style hand-me-downs, antiquities, or anything ethnic will work well, especially in contrast to a modern backdrop. Likewise, contemporary pieces in a historic setting will look singular and impressive. Always try to give decorative storage items visual prominence and space.

above An Oriental-style set of drawers in composite and resin provides distinctive storage for everyday paperwork, videos, and CDs – in contrast to a sandblasted brick interior. (Furniture designer/maker: Andrew Mortada.)

left Ideal for concealing entertainment equipment, a traditional New England cabinet provides essential storage in historic style. In addition to this, a traditional blanket box doubles as both a table and as storage for books and magazines.

right A fork-lift device is in keeping with the size statement of the TV, video, and music system in this New York apartment. A basket for CDs and videos, with black-and-white prints on top, offsets this raw industrial style.

below Compact and mobile, a simple storage system with TV platform, video shelf, and box for tapes can be wheeled into position for viewing when needed. (Biblica from Arc Linea.)

If you enjoy watching TV and videos frequently, invest in a sizeable screen and position it for direct viewing. However, a television that sits directly in front of a sofa or in the center of general living space can conflict with alternative activities and encourage passive, automatic viewing.

Storing entertainment equipment on carts, mobile cabinets, or pivoting wall brackets and moving it into position when you want to use it gives you immediate access along with the flexibility to do something else without effort. Choose a style of storage to fit in with existing decoration – perhaps a lightweight aluminum cart with adjustable shelves, or a low wooden cabinet with a stacking device for TV and VCR and a drawer for video tapes. If you favor stark contrasts between high technology and domesticity, opt for heavy-duty fixtures designed for professional studios.

left Compact music systems on lightweight carts are ideal to move around single-level apartments. Beware of moving music systems with multiple cables. (Habitat.)

right This plastic basket is ideal for transporting CDs. Keep current favorites on view next to a music system for easy access, and store the bulk of a collection elsewhere. (Hold Everything.)

Books are an integral personal feature in any living environment — whether in an informal pile on a chair, on individual shelves arranged in graphic color-coded blocks, or as a random selection in an open storage system alongside artifacts and entertainment equipment. Use adjustable shelving, individual storage cabinets, or modular cabinets that will accommodate anything from standard paperbacks to large format art books. With extensive collections, avoid the overly academic look of book "wallpaper" in a general living area. Instead, partially conceal books behind sliding panels or open and shut storage.

books

above Modular units with open and shut storage can conceal a mass of books and bulky entertainment equipment, while revealing a decorative selection of books and artifacts.

left A bold wooden shelf across an odd space makes a useful and unobtrusive bookshelf. Beware of utilizing every spare bit of space for book storage and thus overpowering a general living area.

above A conventional yet practical storage solution: building a bookcase in an architectural alcove. Use vertical tracks with adjustable shelving for maximum flexibility.

right A country-style wall rack makes convenient storage for magazines, newspapers, and paperbacks. As alternative storage for a selection of books, use a basket or compact cart.

If you can designate space in general living areas for book storage and reading, celebrate with a distinctive storage item – perhaps a rotating book stand or a mobile cabinet with internal shelving; or construct a stack or spiral of inexpensive wooden boxes. Simply stand one on top of the other and let the weight of books act as anchor, or use screws to join them together top and bottom.

Open shelving or low cabinets double as convenient book storage and partitions within open-plan areas. Alternatively, to keep space free and flexible (especially in conventional setups), utilize outer-perimeter storage potential – floor-to-ceiling shelving systems in alcoves or comprehensive wall systems, for example. For a mass of books, store the collection in a shelving system with sliding front panels or doors in wood, metal, or semitransparent glass and reveal different sections at a time. For a similar partial-reveal effect, stretch blank canvas over a light frame and prop it up against conventional book shelves.

left In an open-plan New York apartment, welcoming chairs and a rotating bookstand define a light and spacious reading area.

below Low cabinets
or mobile units such
as this provide convenient
book storage and can also
be used as space dividers
to create a quiet area
for reading.

right A vast Indian bowl
is an imaginative storage
solution for reference
books and magazines,
and sits perfectly between
home office and general
living area.

For a mixture of books and artifacts in open storage, vertical tracks
with adjustable shelves or modular
building-block systems with various
shelving options, provide flexible,
no-fuss solutions.

Tracking systems give maximum
flexibility, especially for large art or
reference books. Alternatively,
install adjustable shelving within a
kit framework. Mount tracks on the
back of the cabinet or side verti-
cals. Use wood for the frame and
either wood, metal, or glass for
shelving. Depending on the size of
the cabinet and load capacity of the
shelving, insert a vertical panel or
track approximately every 20 inches
(50.8 cm). Paint the cabinet (and
back wall), the same color as the
rest of the room to throw books
and artifacts into relief. Or decorate to emphasize the frame, not
the shelf positions within. Perhaps
use contrasting paint colors for
frame and shelving or mount archi-
traving or facing on the frame.

left Books and artifacts on open shelving
provide a decorative display. Paint units the
same color as the surrounding walls to offset
ceramics and pieces of art.

right A contemporary version of a cinderblock
and plank shelf construction is collapsible and
extendable horizontally and vertically with aluminum connector brackets. (Design: Ali Tayar.)

bedroom

left A wall of built-in closets – with wallcovering and paneling to match the rest of the room – provides extensive invisible bedroom storage.

the closet

left An ornate metal frame with drapes makes decorative freestanding storage. As an alternative to metal, put together a simple wooden frame or box and hang plain canvas banners all around.

above This expandable flexible storage system – with basic steel frame, shelf, and clothes rod fronted by a curtain pole and cotton drapes – provides ample hanging and shelf space.

right A substantial storage solution that makes use of built-in closets on either side of a window. Natural Roman shades, instead of traditional doors, hide clothes and shoes.

Creating the right environment for sleep and relaxation is very important – so plan bedroom storage with special care and attention to detail. If space is at a premium and a bedroom is also an office, gym, or alternative television room, then organization and flexible storage are especially critical. The closet is usually the central storage item in the bedroom. A mixture of hanging and drawer or shelf space will provide all the basic storage requirements for clothing. Take into account the ratio of hanging space to shelf space available, together with the overall space and structure or architecture of the environment, to find a workable storage solution.

A single storage network of inexpensive self-assembly metal, composite board, or pine drawers with basic hanging rods and adjustable shelving systems can provide complete bedroom storage. Arrange the network along one wall or divide it between two alcoves. Contain everything in an overall framework and conceal with sliding panels, doors, or a curtain on a metal pole.

Individual storage sections can be concealed in different ways – for example, hang a linen shade in front of shelves, leave a section of baskets or storage boxes on view, and install a sliding mirror panel in front of clothes rods. In period-style interiors where the walls are decorated with paneling or wallpaper, match the closet fronts to the rest of the scheme, continue any architrave or baseboard, and create an invisible wall of storage.

Open storage for clothing is another option, and is ideal for minimalists or anyone who favors a strict color code. Avoid overloading open rails, or clashing colors and patterns – the effect can be chaotic. Clothing bags or canvas or plastic bags with front zippers will help reduce the jumbled effect and protect clothes from dust.

above A metal frame cabinet with deep drawers provides ample storage for underwear, sweaters, shirts, and jeans. Each drawer can be lined with tissue paper to help keep clothes pristine.

below Storing out-of-season sweaters and shirts in a transparent envelope will protect them from dust in a drawer or open shelf. Bags with canvas backing help clothes "breathe."

above As an original alternative to clothes rods running parallel to a wall, these head-on clear plastic rods provide compact storage.

right Functional and stylish open storage with clear plastic rods and sculptural shelf, inspired by Gabriella Ligenza's London hat shop fittings. Plastic boxes store special items on the top shelf. (Design: Janie Jackson.)

Choose high-quality fittings and fixtures such as sculptural shelves, plastic clothes rods, or metal structures for distinctive open bedroom storage. Supplement minimalist clothes rods with additional storage for everyday sweaters, shirts, and underwear; a simple line of open baskets, an independent set of drawers, or accessible shelves will work well. Cardboard or plastic boxes with lids, impractical for everyday use, are ideal for storing less frequently worn or out-of-season clothes.

Explore the possibility of installing compact sets of drawers, or shelves that will hold a line of boxes or baskets, within existing closets. Characterful period pieces such as armoires, with only a single rod or three or four shelves, can be imaginatively refitted to provide ample storage. Incorporate space-saving devices like a spinning tie-rack on a hook or hang shoe organizers or bags inside doors.

For any additional bedroom storage, offset period pieces with contemporary items such as a Plexiglas trolley with drawers. Be creative when mixing styles and sizes, and consider painting or silver-leafing dark wood pieces to lighten any grandiose effect.

left A compact tie spinner neatly stores ties. Utilize small-scale storage solutions like this to improve organization and protect clothing within traditional or contemporary closets.

right An architectural metal structure at one end of this bedroom provides hanging space for suit bags with cheap and cheerful brown paper bags below for underwear, sweaters, and T-shirts. (Design: Justin Meath Baker.)

below Moroccan-style drapes and a kilim transform a simple alcove closet into a striking feature. If possible, install a wall or ceiling light when partitioning walk-in storage space.

left Voluminous drawstring sacks with contrasting interlinings make jolly storage for toys. They are easy to carry from one play area to another and ideal for a quick toy sweep when play is over.

right and below An inventive twist on underbed storage: a bed that pulls out from and stores away underneath a magnificent glass display platform revealing a collection of sea treasures. The room has ample storage for clothing in lockers and hung from clothes rods. This is a compact and inventive design solution that downplays the bed as a dominant feature of the room without major disruption or effort. (Architectural design: Charles Rutherfoord.)

bed and
bedside

The style, size, and position of a bed is a key factor in organizing space and planning storage solutions in a sleeping environment. Flexible bedroom furniture, such as roll-up futons, beds that hinge or pivot out of the way, sofabeds, or bed platforms, can provide valuable extra storage space. But there are many alternative simple storage ideas, often centered under or beside the bed, that suit conventional arrangements and maximize the sense of space.

right Decorative chairs provide simple storage for everyday clothing and clean laundry. With ample storage elsewhere, witty details like this enliven an interior.

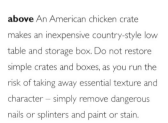

above An American chicken crate makes an inexpensive country-style low table and storage box. Do not restore simple crates and boxes, as you run the risk of taking away essential texture and character – simply remove dangerous nails or splinters and paint or stain.

right A cast-off display cabinet fits conveniently beneath a window to provide expansive storage space in the bedroom. The contents can be partly concealed by stapling muslin or linen over glass panels, or replacing clear glass with sand-blasted glass.

Many contemporary bed designs integrate storage space for essential items. Space for books and reading lamps can be found within headboards, swivel side tables, or vast mattress platforms with runaround, benchlike shelves. For a simple headboard and shelf combination, set a divan or bed base away from the wall, run two long shelves behind it extending on each side of the base, then insert a masonite panel between the bed base and shelves. Place one shelf level with the bed base and one just below the top of the panel. Paint everything one color and slide the bed base up against the panel. Use the top shelf for storing books or to prop up a favorite painting. Use the lower shelf, concealed behind the masonite panel, for storing infrequently used items.

As an alternative to traditional pieces such as blanket boxes, use wicker hampers or travel chests to store spare pillows and out-of-season comforters. Look out for quirky used display cabinets and line glass panels with muslin or gauze.

left An architectural recess shelf above this bed provides storage for bedside essentials, in addition to swivel side tables. Clothing is housed in a mobile closet with aluminum doors. (Furniture from Ligne Roset.)

Utilizing space under a bed for practical storage is worth every effort. Even if saving space is a not an issue, exploit the potential to store substantial amounts of clothing, bedding, or equipment conveniently out of sight.

Built-in drawers in bed frames can provide expansive underbed storage – ideal for shirts, sweaters, spare bed linen, and blankets. If space is tight and side drawers are inconvenient, put drawers at the foot of the bed for easier access.

As an alternative to built-in storage, combine any high-level bed with independent low-level storage. A wooden platform (or possibly even a single drawer from a pine chest) on heavy-duty castors provides a perfect base for storage. Either place items directly onto the platform, or store within open boxes or baskets on top of the platform.

Use boxes with lids to protect clothes from dust, and store sweaters and shirts in transparent clothes bags in open baskets or containers; use muslin drawstring liners and seal individual piles, or simply place a linen napkin or towel on top. For stability, anchor the containers to the platform or platforms with screws or glue.

above A custom-built bed with large underbed drawers for shirts, T-shirts, sweaters, and spare bed linen makes the most of otherwise "dead" space. Two distinctive bedside cabinets, one a practical cube design and one artistic and decorative, complete this idiosyncratic scheme. (Design: Justin Meath Baker.)

right A bed on a scaffolding frame sits high enough for easy underbed access. Canvas containers on wheels provide useful additional storage for clothing and blankets.

left Open canvas or cardboard boxes are ideal for underbed storage. To protect clothing from dust, use transparent plastic bags or containers.

bathroom

Include storage ideas at the planning stage of any new bath or shower room. A simple recess shelf in the wall of the shower area for gels and lotions is integral to the design and space in a way that a soap-on-a-rope hanging on a nozzle is not. If you plan to conceal pipework with a false wall, continue the false wall to the ceiling and create a recessed shelving system that you can either leave open or conceal with a sliding mirror panel or mirror doors.

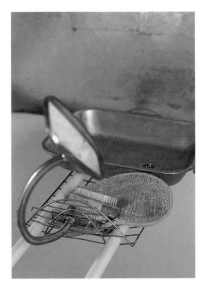

left This bath rack cleverly uses everyday items. A draining rack and roasting pan sit on plastic poles with a flexible rear-view mirror and provide no-fuss storage for a daily shave. (Design: Justin Meath Baker.)

towels and
toiletries

left This metal basket allows a bar of soap to drain and sits at an angle for easy access. As long as soap is not swimming in a puddle of water, any small pot, bowl, or basket will work well.

left A perfect compact arrangement for people who get soap in their eyes. Everything is conveniently on hand, from underbasin cabinet to toothbrush rack and linen bag – all in period style.

above Concealing hot and cold water pipes and the toilet cistern behind wood paneling provides a useful run-around shelf for bowls, boxes, mirror, and bathroom cabinet.

Standing at a basin to wash requires immediate access to essential items in a compact space — from soap, nailbrush, and toothbrush to washcloths and towels. The advantage of basins with built-in surrounds—anything from an architectural piece of glass or slab of stone to a traditional washstand with a basin set into wood or marble—is that essential items are all within easy reach. The main disadvantage is that excessive splashing will soak everything.

To keep soap or wooden brushes from sitting in a puddle of water, store them in a wire basket or use traditional marble dishes with drainage holes. Drain toothbrushes by standing them in a metal or glass tumbler. For an ad hoc solution, use a sculptural stainless steel colander and store everything together. It is a pity to use only specialist bathroom fixtures like chrome toothbrush holders or soap dishes on wall brackets when often a favorite bowl or something basic from the kitchen will provide effective storage with originality.

right A sculptural basin and surround present an imaginative storage solution for soaps and lotions. Glass shelves above the bathtub provide backup storage for additional items. (Architects: Munkenbeck + Marshall.)

left In this compact bathroom, simple storage items include basic soap dish, mirror cabinet, and shelf. Towels and clothing hang on a heated towel rod beside the door. Architects: (Munkenbeck + Marshall.)

right Hanging cylindrical canvas sacks provide useful additional storage on the back of a door. Simply thread plastic-coated garden wire through drawstring bags, make a wire loop at one end, and hang on simple hooks.

Shelves and cabinets above basins provide practical eye-level storage. Do not limit yourself to bathroom-specific versions. Consider stainless steel racks from kitchen suppliers, wood and metal food lockers, or simple open shelf systems, and use as inexpensive alternatives to standard metal or wood mirrored-door cabinets. Hang a plain mirror above a basin with shelf brackets on each side, and use driftwood, slate, or copper sheeting for inexpensive individual shelving.

If a basin stands in front of a window, use the windowsill or install a single shelf below the window frame. As an alternative, stretch high-tension wire across the window frame, using eye plates and a wire tensioner (from sports equipment suppliers), and hook up a mirror and wire basket for toothbrushes, soap, and washcloths.

A cabinet under a basin is a very logical use of space. It can conceal pipework and provides ample hideaway storage. Use it to store special items, backup supplies, and cleaning materials.

left Japanese bathing principles in a workshop conversion include cedar bath and separate shower for washing hidden behind a mosaic panel. A simple set of drawers and wall of cabinets store towels and cleaning materials.

Part of the pleasure of getting in a bathtub is not getting out again until you choose to. Store essentials and lotions within easy reach of the tub. The simplest storage solution is a rack that fits across the tub or a series of metal baskets that hang over the side. An inexpensive basket or bucket hanging on a faucet will work just as well.

If you plan to enclose a bathtub, aim to incorporate a wide storage shelf – ideally all around the tub or, if space is tight, on one side or one end. If the bathtub is set against a wall, insert a series of hooks along the wall just above the level of the bath and store supplies in a row of small baskets. A folding chair can provide temporary storage beside the bath.

Shower enclosures require no-fuss storage solutions. Plan any storage at the design stage if possible and incorporate an alcove in the wet area for shower gels and shampoo, and a dry area for towels and clothing. For example, a shelf above the shower head or, in a compact space, a plastic box with a lid will keep essentials dry. In simple enclosures, shower racks hanging on a hook or over a temperature control switch will store gels, soap, and brushes within easy reach.

right Incorporate storage ideas at the planning stage of a new bathroom, like this colorful tongue-and-groove plan with built-in bath and shelf surround and recess with glass shelves. (Design: Justin Meath Baker.)

below Simple metal loops for towels, clothes, and bathrobe augment a traditional kitchen chair for practical storage. On bathtubs with sloping sides, a run-around rod is ideal for hanging bath towels. (Design: Philippe Starck for Duravit.)

right Internal shelves in a deep curving bathroom door create inventive storage boxes for toiletries, books, and loofahs. As an alternative, hang a line of bicycle baskets or plastic containers down the middle of a plain door for easy access. A round basin cabinet provides contrasting hideaway storage. (Design: Justin Meath Baker.)

kitchen

ergonomics

With resourceful planning it is possible to design an informal, user-friendly kitchen with a minimum of fuss and expense. Begin with a review of basic appliances and storage requirements. Draw a map or plan of your existing kitchen, plot any changes or additions on paper, and re-use or reorganize anything you can. A few simple adjustments can make all the difference to day-to-day efficiency and practicality.

above Hanging wall cabinets are the main feature of this food preparation area. Pull-out box drawers house pans and utensils. (Design: Rick Baker.)

below A contemporary stainless steel rail in this Japanese kitchen echoes the style of a traditional American Shaker design and provides good eye-level storage.

above Making the most of available light and space under a roof, everything is close at hand in this kitchen. Cabinets pull out to provide extra surfaces for food preparation. (Design: Justin Meath Baker.)

above Inexpensive zinc sheets held in place with glue and upholstery tacks transform basic cabinets. Bright paintwork inside the cabinets, and hand-crafted pulls complete an inspiring make-over. (Design: Justin Meath Baker.)

right In this New York loft, open shelving holds pans, china, and glassware, while a row of cabinets underneath provides good-looking storage for kitchen basics. Specialist utensils and equipment are stacked neatly under walk-around tables.

A new relaxation about food preparation, a preference for sharing informal meals in the kitchen with family and friends, and a demand for simple environments signal a change in kitchen design and storage style. This keep-it-simple approach adapts easily to any style. So work within an existing architectural framework, apply simple ergonomics, and update any kitchen to a functional and welcoming space.

Before you go ahead with a major reorganization, run a quick check on all equipment, utensils, and tableware. Divide everything into essential items for accessible storage and nonessential items. Use this opportunity to remove any duplicates or extinct items. Why keep identical cheese graters or a rusty wok? Be realistic about storage options. Set a budget and invest in workable solutions that fit all individual requirements. There is no point buying an expensive, good-looking system with inadequate storage space. Also, it is important to avoid overcrowding – for safety reasons and for efficiency.

left In this dynamic conversion of a 19th-century workshop, a steel bar full of hanging pans and utensils means that all essential cooking items are close at hand.

For an efficient kitchen, begin with the position of basic appliances. Provide storage for cookware and tableware within an arm's span of key work stations and activity areas – so, store pots and pans next to a cooking appliance and knives and chopping board next to a work surface. Store tableware next to a sink, dishwasher, or table.

Storage possibilities are limitless, ranging from an informal combination of freestanding furniture, open shelving, and hanging racks to a system of built-in cabinets. The key factor in choosing effort-saving solutions is proximity. A drawer under a cooking appliance for pots and pans, pull-out baskets for food storage next to a work surface, or a wall rack beside a sink for clean china and glassware, all provide simple storage and upgrade kitchen efficiency. In a one-wall line-up with all appliances and storage together, the big issue is space-saving flexible storage. Compact options include pull-out shelf racks for food, deep drawers for cookware and tableware, a hanging rack for pots and pans, and a wheel-out cabinet or trolley with work surface and shelves underneath. Any remaining space is free for a table and chairs and general living space.

above A wooden wall slides across to enclose a kitchen, leaving the refrigerator/freezer in the dining area. Behind panels, this appliance is unobtrusive in an open-plan setting. (Architects: Munkenbeck + Marshall.)

left Plain, functional, and well put together, this kitchen in an open-plan New York apartment illustrates the fine art of low-key storage.

right Basic white cabinets provide floor-level storage, practical for heavy items such as cleaning equipment and saucepans, as well as creating a strong base for a joint counter and kitchen table.

on display

Matter-of-fact storage solutions – from rustic baskets and mason jars to on-view collections of utensils or everyday foodstuffs – can add vitality and color to functional catering environments. Simple details such as a line of cooking oils or preserves on a stainless steel shelf or a stack of favorite mixing bowls on a plain counter will enliven any space. Open kitchen storage, with everyday items within easy reach, is perfect for busy cooks.

left In this compact country kitchen, a simple shelf, plastic plate rack, and swivel dish towel rod allows easy access.

below Crisscross stainless steel shelves with open brackets take up less visual space than conventional wooden versions. (Shelves from Slingsby.)

above Economy of effort is often a result of having essential utensils close at hand. This rustic flatware box is perfect for the middle of the table for everyday meals.

right An attractive raised-pattern tray carries espresso cups to the dining table and also acts as a portable makeshift draining board when it is lined with paper towels.

A kitchen with its workings and contents on view is a welcoming place and, crucially, everything is highly accessible.

Typical storage solutions include basic utensils in ceramic pots; various rush baskets full of fresh vegetables, fruit, and eggs; jars of preserves displayed on shelves; and orderly stacks of cooking pots and bowls on a workbench or table. Perhaps as a backlash to laboratory-type kitchens, this tradition of presenting a visual index of essentials and things in store is back in favor. In moderation, and with twists to update this look, open storage translates well to even the most minimalist of kitchens.

Simplicity is the key. Avoid the confusion and chaos of taking everything you have out of the pantry and into the open. Instead, include only essential items in frequent use. Bear in mind that accessibility is as crucial as the visual effect. There is little point storing mason jars three-deep on a shelf, or putting your favorite salad bowl under a stack of heavy cookware so that it is difficult to remove.

left An out-of-service Dualit toaster is given shelf space as a rack for saucepan lids, while a galvanized bucket from a hardware store acts as a practical and generous utensil container.

An "open" kitchen can present many opportunities for creative storage ideas. Kitchen utensils can be stored in tool boxes, or even something as basic as a tin bucket or a terra-cotta plant pot. By pooling together odds and ends, clutter can be eliminated. A white pitcher with a selection of favorite wooden implements or an Oriental basket or steamer holding a jumble of cooking oils, spice jars, and herbs looks efficient and hardworking if placed next to the stove.

Kitchens with an emphasis on display are convenient for busy cooks who need to have everything at hand. For unusual ad hoc storage solutions, choose whatever items fit the environment. A sudden contrast—perhaps an African basket in a marble and stainless-steel kitchen—will look over-exotic. In general, resourceful yet compatible storage works best: Provençal storage jars and creamware pitchers for rustics, white ceramics and maple baskets for purists, and metal beakers or glass tank vases for modernists.

left Good accessibility is the feature of this kitchen storage solution. Equipment for food preparation or cooking is neatly stacked and clearly in view. This is no-fuss storage for people who like to cook.

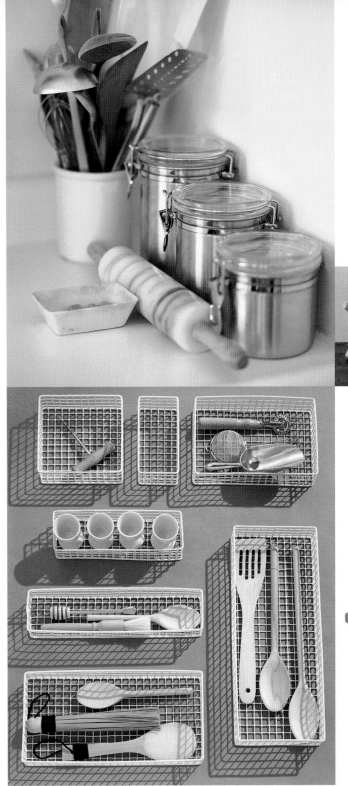

left An orderly line of stainless steel and glass jars in different sizes provides convenient storage for everyday essentials including coffee and sugar.

below A foldaway two-tier plate rack in stainless steel and wood helps to drain and store china, glasses, and flatware.

left Individual lift-out containers inside kitchen drawers separate different types of utensils and prevent the usual jumble of everything thrown together.

below A mobile work surface with wide drawer, towel rods, and adjustable shelves is ideal for wheeling into action when needed, then storing out of the way.

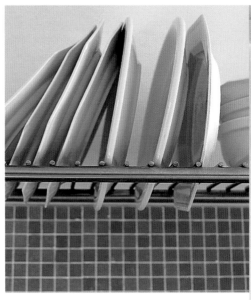

left This is functional yet decorative storage. Secure a firm anchor for butcher's hooks in an exposed beam or wooden rod and hook up kitchen utensils and earthenware pots.

above A stainless steel rack above a work surface. With a mosaic tile area below, it is ideal for draining as well as storing plates.

below Stainless steel bars give this modern kitchen a professional catering look: convenient for drainage, quick access, and for hooking up pots and pans.

right A series of parallel steel rods fitted with hooks provide compact storage for pans, skillets, and utensils. (Architects: Solveig Fernlund & Neil Logan.)

lofty
ideas

A simple hook can have a big impact upon the efficiency of a kitchen – in a way that expensive storage solutions and kitchen designs often do not. Everyday utensils and pans hanging within easy reach of a cooking surface symbolize a cook at work. Hooks and hanging rods provide logical and functional no-fuss storage for working kitchens.

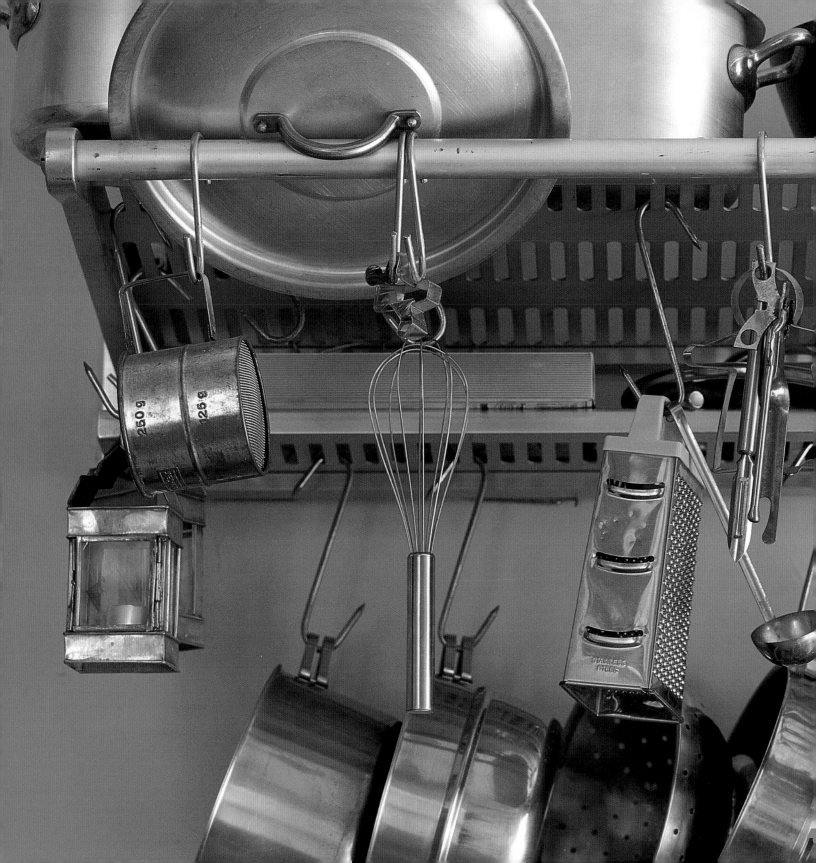

Hooks and hanging rods, with a jumble of pans and utensils, offer an anti-order storage option. There are no cabinet doors to open or slide out of the way, and no place for artifice or to display items that collect dust—just sensible storage for everyday equipment

Before you opt for this level of exposure, lay out everything you plan to hang up. Divide up and position items according to function in the kitchen; for example, place cups by the coffee maker and pans and utensils by the stove. Take a look at how much there is to hang (allow for a few acquisitions over time) and figure out where everything can go.

Use hooks, hanging rods, or frames. Simple hooks work well for small items such as earthenware pitchers or aprons and dishtowels. Rods and frames are ideal for pans and utensils. Good anchorage to a wall or beam is critical, especially if you plan to hang everything with a handle from a single steel rod. Hanging frames, perhaps above a work surface, will distribute weight evenly.

left A luggage rack from a train provides versatile storage for kitchen utensils. With scope to hook up baskets for added small-scale storage, it makes a striking display.

left A washing machine, drier, refrigerator, freezer, and set of pull-out food racks form a precise geometric arrangement in this kitchen. Swing-open doors provide easy access to laundry appliances and conceal control panels. (Architect: Gunnar Orefelt.)

right Opaque Plexiglas panels create a seamless line from standard kitchen cabinets and basic appliances. A continuous counter and mosaic splashback complete the architectural simplicity of the scheme. (Architects: Munkenbeck + Marshall.)

below A spacious drawer underneath an oven and range provides ample storage for roasting pans, baking sheets, and large chopping boards. The wood-veneer finish on the drawer coordinates with kitchen cabinets throughout.

appliances

Raw kitchen appliances can look out of place within a coordinating kitchen, so storage is a critical factor. Replace or install fascia panels on appliance doors to conceal standard fixtures and unify a design scheme. Store laundry appliances in a separate area, or fit them into standard kitchen cabinet frames with swing-open doors to reduce noise levels and hide control panels. Check ventilation and plumbing requirements before committing to any changes.

utility room

right This compact canvas and metal frame laundry basket for bathrooms and bedrooms is a welcome update on conventional Alibaba baskets.

left The luxury and convenience of a traditional built-in storage cupboard is shown off in this London townhouse. Narrow shelves inside provide ample storage space for bed linen, towels, and essential supplies. (Design: Eliza Cairns.)

cleaning and
laundry

Without labor-saving ideas and good storage solutions, cleaning and laundry can be a real chore. Simple ideas, such as storing laundry detergent on a shelf above a washing machine and sorting cleaning equipment into individual buckets for particular cleaning tasks, can minimize effort. Flexible options such as folding laundry carts and pull-up ceiling racks provide instant storage. Likewise, pull-out and wheel-around kitchen cabinets with shelves for cleaning equipment or an ironing board on a permanent pull-down wall installation, provide flexible storage to increase efficiency and convenience.

above In this compact utility area, all the essentials are stored within easy reach. Restaurant canisters hold detergents and related items, while buckets are housed under the sink.

right Wheel out this professional metal container on washdays for storing substantial laundry bundles. It is also useful for transporting cleaning equipment. (From Slingsby.)

above This foldaway lightweight laundry cart with removable stringmesh bag and wheels is ideal for collecting and storing wash or general household items. (From Slingsby.)

right A sculptural shopping cart is perfectly compatible with the sandblasted glass partitions and industrial fixtures in this schoolhouse conversion. Its graphic profile compensates for its basic function of storing bathroom supplies.

below Once a clothing locker at a New York public swimming pool, this wire basket is convenient for storing spare candles and specialized cleaning equipment for silverware. Use any wicker basket or container in this way.

right The front of this mobile kitchen cabinet flips down to reveal a plastic trash can. Inside, a network of different shelves provide specific storage for cleaning rags and food storage bags. (Design: Justin Meath Baker.)

For the storage of large-scale cleaning and laundry equipment, like vacuum cleaners and ironing boards, decide on a single cabinet if you can, and keep everything in one place for convenience. Arrange equipment so that heavy items are directly on the floor and nearest the door to save unnecessary lifting. For cleaning equipment with long tubing, remove the plastic hose and hang it over a nail or hook. Brooms and mops can be hung on the inside of the door. Buy the sort that have a handle with a hole in the top, or drill a hole in the top and thread a loop of string or tape to hook onto hardware on the wall.

Buckets provide perfect storage for cleaning rags, liquid sprays, and polish. Store everything in one bucket and simply take it with you on your chores. In addition to being portable, buckets can hang out of the way or stack on top of each other to save space. Pick up laundry in mobile foldaway containers, or line conventional laundry baskets with laundry bags and simply remove the bag full of laundry on washdays.

right An inexpensive plastic container with handle is handy for heavy-duty cleaning. Replace the lid for practical permanent storage for rags, trash can liners, and liquid sprays.

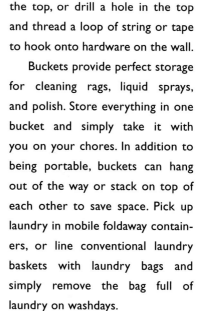

home office

right Multi-drawer units such as this wire system provide storage for essential office items. Invent a quick-search system by attaching photographs of what is inside on the front of each drawer.

left Good-sized baskets in metal make ideal portable storage containers for paperwork or files. Look out for ex-industrial metal trays in office warehouse sales or seek out exotic grocery boxes.

pen and
paper

below Library and department-store style are combined in these traditional storage items. Such pieces do not look out of place in modern home offices.

right A Mexican table, sculptural metal stools, an original clothes locker from a public swimming pool, and metal jars for pens and pencils provide stylish basics for a daytime office area at one end of this New York apartment. (Design: C.I.T.E.)

above Precision building-block units for equipment and information storage coordinate to individual specifications to provide flexible add-on home office storage.

right In any office in a home environment, special human elements, like this collection of Oriental baskets for storing pencils and elastic bands, will serve to offset worklike precision and conformity.

Working from home is now a viable empowering option for many people. The rapid expansion in communication networks, inexpensive computer systems, and new thinking about how, where, and when we work all contribute to this change. Yet setting up an office at home can create unique problems. Organization with flexibility and imaginative storage is the key to success in any environment.

If you opt to work from home, aim to take over a whole room and set it up as a welcoming, ready-to-use environment. There is no reason for this space to look like a conventional office, and as it is self-contained you will not be restricted to fitting in with design decisions elsewhere in the house. However, it is possible that you will have to use an area within an established room for your home office. The main consideration with dual-function environments is how to organize space and store equipment without compromising work or living activities.

Apart from essential investments such as excellent seating, a solid work surface, good basic equipment, and lighting, this is an ideal opportunity to invest in creative storage solutions. Mix industrial shelving with metal cupboards and mobile sets of drawers in low-key industrial style; perhaps opt for a traditional oak desk with library shelves and consider commissioning a custom-built system of storage cabinets and work surface or choose specialized items from contract suppliers.

right In a New York apartment, a modernist red table effectively frames and diffuses the raw industrial feel of an assertive line-up of heavy-duty metal filing cabinets. (Design: C.I.T.E.)

Whether your idea of an essential work space is a computer terminal with fax, answering machine, and coffee maker, or a plain table with a sheet of paper and a pencil, ample storage will prevent an office from taking over a domestic set-up.

Open-plan interiors offer many possibilities for delineating office space. Partitions or storage units can divide working and living areas. For conventional dual-function areas (a kitchen table, bedroom alcove, or hallway), reorganize existing storage or introduce mobile storage cabinets. Alternatively, choose new cabinets with ample storage potential in a style that is in keeping with existing surroundings. A metal front-opening travel trunk, an Indian temple cupboard, Shaker-style kitchen cabinet, or modular wall units all provide functional options and fit in with contemporary interiors. For fax machines, small printers, and photocopiers, sturdy trolleys in metal, plastic, or wood are the best option. The simpler the storage solution, the quicker the transition from work space to living space, and vice versa.

above In an open-plan New York apartment, an antique desk and modern plastic trolley provide ample storage and work space.

left Good organization and under-desk storage limits the impact of essential computer equipment and office paperwork upon living space.

right Mobile storage cabinets can wheel in and out to screen office activities during working hours. (Mobile unit from Driade.)

right Built in a prime position in good light, this flip-down desk makes clever use of space. Cabinets below and on each side provide storage for books, files, and a fax machine.

small-scale storage

small-scale
storage

Finding storage solutions for small-scale essentials will revolutionize the way you live with a new sense of order. Avoid convention and use kitchen items in bathrooms for storing sponges, soaps, and body brushes; introduce office surplus into bedrooms for socks, underwear, and accessories; and bring plant pots into kitchens to store stainless steel and wooden utensils. As well as providing decorative and personal storage, explore the hidden possibilities of plastic boxes as drawer dividers and baskets inside cabinets for extra efficiency and a welcome sense of space.

above A simple metal basket makes a convenient organizer for kitchen sink clutter, such as washing brushes, cloths, and liquids. Use a separate basket for storing clean cutlery or vegetable brushes.

right Any size or shape of rustic basket provides ideal storage in a country-style interior. Hang them from simple nails or hooks in kitchens, bathrooms, or hallways for household essentials.

left Inexpensive Oriental baskets, like this Chinese vegetable steamer (available from specialized supermarkets or kitchen suppliers), can be easily upgraded to become decorative storage items.

above Store everyday kitchen utensils in simple open baskets for order and accessibility. Teaspoons can be placed alongside a kettle, while cooking oils and utensils can sit next to a cooking surface.

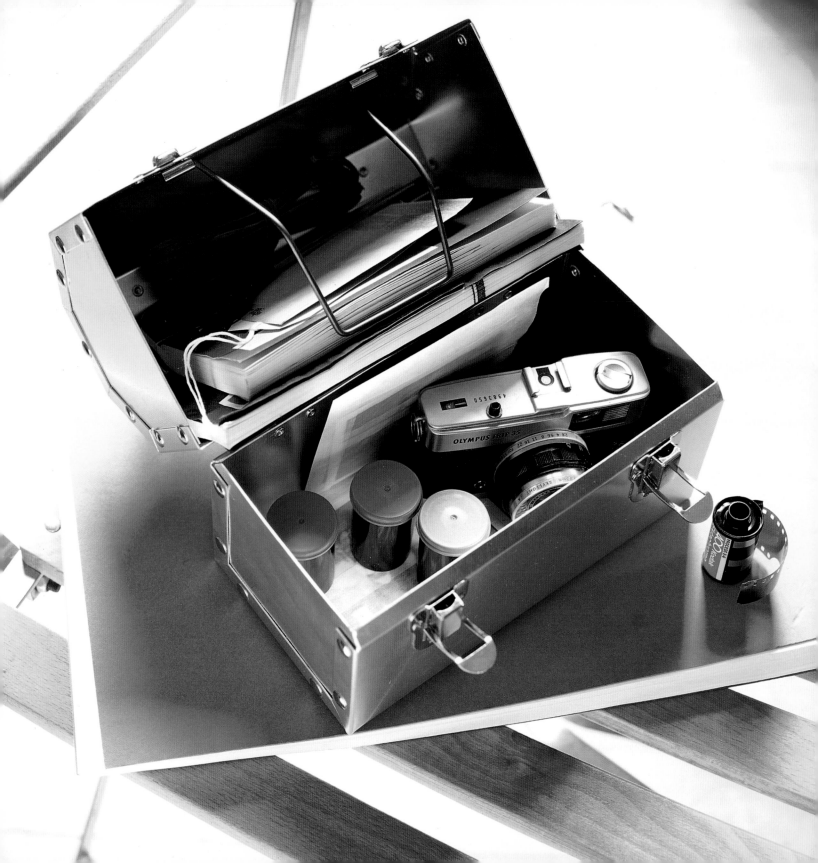

left Sweep up any random collections of vacation photographs, household bills and documents, or CDs in multi-use cardboard and metal storage boxes. They are ideal for visible stacks on tables or on open shelving systems, inside closets or under beds. (Boxes from Muji.)

right Pull-out boxes for sewing kits or baskets for knitting provide lightweight portable storage. Use containers with pulls and devise an easy-reference labeling system – perhaps plastic bags stuck to the front with a sample of the contents.

left Metal or plastic lunch boxes make versatile and protective storage for special interest items such as camera equipment or art materials. For alternative hard-wearing storage containers, check office suppliers for petty-cash boxes, mini-safes, and filing boxes.

Boxes eliminate the visual clutter of collections of small-scale items and provide efficient storage solutions for everyday requirements, from a stack of CDs to household documents. Use plastic or cardboard open boxes for organizing the inside of cabinets; ideal for piles of T-shirts, table linen, or toys. Store boxes along the bottom of a cabinet or on basic shelving for easy access. For dust-free storage of fragile clothing, computer disks, or any paraphernalia not in everyday circulation, use boxes with lids.

As a low-cost do-it-yourself storage system, mount a series of parallel shelves on the wall to provide a basic framework. Then fill in rows of boxes. Install optional side panels for extra definition or even construct a free-standing frame on wheels. Either way, keep the top shelf clear for opening and sorting individual boxes. Design a quick-reference labeling system, perhaps luggage tags, colored adhesive labels, letters of the alphabet, or numbers. As an alternative, you can use a selection of semitransparent plastic boxes so you can see the individual contents at a glance.

Although there is a wide selection of specialty products and designs to match small-scale storage requirements for bathrooms, it is worth looking beyond the conventional choices and putting together an eclectic mixture of essentials with wit and originality.

Stick to basics if you want a contemporary style. Plain white china mugs, bowls, glass tumblers, and metal beakers provide low-cost storage for toothbrushes, natural sponges, and soaps. Often, a simple change of environment for familiar household objects is enough to create a new look.

Cosmetics and cotton balls can be stored in transparent pencil cases, food jars with snap-lids, and even in plastic food boxes. Use glass flower vases for body brushes and loofahs and frosty dessert dishes for soaps. Convert bubble-glass cooking oil jars and miniature spice jars into decorative storage for lotions and homemade aromatic bath oils.

left Simple white china, glass, and metal containers from the kitchen transfer to bathrooms for simple storage. Add a favorite decorative piece to enliven and personalize a basic lineup.

right Bring decorative garden urns and plant pots indoors for imaginative storage solutions. Also, mix together wire boxes, plant containers, and stone pots.

above Inexpensive terra-cotta pots and earthenware storage jars work well with period fittings and add color and texture to country-style bathrooms.

right Empty jelly jars or mason jars with snap-lids provide inexpensive solutions for keeping together essential odds and ends such as pencils, rubber bands, stamps, and paper clips.

Reinvent, recycle, and reuse familiar household items as alternative storage solutions. For example, transfer talcum powder to a sugar shaker for easy sprinkling, keep household receipts, take-out menus, and timetables on an office-surplus clipboard and hang it up on the back of a cabinet door; or reuse cardboard shoe boxes for photographs or stationery supplies.

Recycle jelly jars, plastic food containers, and cookie tins for convenient airtight food storage. Hardware stores and office suppliers are a good source for a mass of ad hoc storage items. Use expandable toolboxes for toiletries, cosmetics, or a sewing kit, or convert plastic mini drawer-systems, originally for screws and nails, for cotton swabs, tweezers, and nail scissors. Also, colorful petty-cash boxes or safes are ideal as jewelry boxes; metal or plastic paper trays work well as storage for belts and scarves, and wastepaper baskets are useful for keeping magazines and newspapers orderly in living environments.

right For low-cost storage, recycle food cans for pens and pencils, fabric swatches, or darning thread. Use a can opener to remove any sharp edges and wash the can thoroughly.

below Stacks of colorful rustic boxes provide decorative storage in both country-style and contemporary interiors.

right The simplicity and honesty of Shaker boxes can offset machine-age entertainment equipment in multi-functional living environments.

left Mix and match a collection of ethnic baskets for decorative color-coded storage on open shelving.

right A used swimsuit mannequin is an unusual hanging frame for kitchen mugs. Explore the possibilities of topiary frames in sculptural or animal shapes for a similar decorative display.

Transposing historic or ethnic storage items into contemporary settings can provide new storage possibilities far away from the original commonplace use.

Historic Shaker boxes, made by craftspeople for storing everyday kitchen and workshop items, now look out of place in workaday situations. Antique country boxes, earthenware or stone storage jars, milk pitchers, and medicine jars, once seen as functional items, are too precious for kitchen or household items. Use these storage treasures for jewelry, mementos, and anything of personal value. For decorative general storage, look to ethnic basketware and simple wooden boxes. Often inexpensive yet with fine detailing or craftwork, they are ideal for many practical storage applications. Use colorful African market baskets, originally used for carrying fruit and vegetables, to store clothing and magazines, and Oriental vegetable steamers or sisal spice baskets for cosmetics and toiletries.

Viewed with imagination, many antique items that were not originally designed for the purpose can also provide decorative storage. For example, antique hats can hold cosmetics, scarves, and belts.

yard and garage

storage
shelters

Garden sheds and garages require common-sense storage solutions. Gardening is a hands-on outdoor activity that begins with a visit to a shed, or possibly a shelf, to pick up your equipment. Apart from a table or counter for repotting or sharpening tools, a single row of long nails will provide no-fuss storage for hanging spades, rakes, and forks. A galvanized trash can will prevent fertilizers and plant food from drying out or getting too damp. In sizeable yards, a wheelbarrow is useful for transporting equipment, while a gardening apron with pockets is handy for compact tools.

above An outdoor peg rail under the shelter of an overhanging roof makes orderly storage for gardening tools, plant box, and wicker basket. A line of nails will work as well.

left A slatted wooden shelf on bracket mounts makes a simple, well-drained potting table with space to store various plants and galvanized florist's buckets.

left A traditional wicker gardener's basket sports sturdy handle and straps to hold tools and gardening gloves in place. With space for plants, seeds, or bulbs, it is a practical companion for any gardener.

left A rustproof galvanized can provides effective outdoor storage for a compact town garden. With room for a watering can, garden tools, fertilizers, and string, it is full without being chaotic or unworkable.

In garages, even with a car inside, there is ample storage potential on walls and ceilings. For sports equipment such as skis or bicycles, invest in specialized wall or ceiling brackets available from sports suppliers. Alternatively, for a bicycle, secure firm hardware for two heavy-duty shelf brackets and support the frame under the crossbar or below the seat and handle bars. For rackets, bats, balls, and sports shoes, put up a high-level shelf – a wooden rack on brackets or a series of wooden or metal parallel poles stretching across one wall with occasional brackets underneath for extra support. Hang hooks on the poles for additional storage of gardening implements or sports clothing.

For tools and household maintenance and decorating equipment, metal filing cabinets with good-sized drawers for cans of paint and electrical tools are in keeping with the workaday look of a garage environment. Plastic boxes and blockboard shelves or self-assembly cabinets work well for a mix of different tools, cans, and essentials.

left A self-assembly modular cabinet, with optional doors and shelf components, stores tools and equipment and provides a strong base for a work table. (From Cubestore.)

above Former household or broken items often resurface in tool sheds or garages as ad hoc storage solutions. This split flatware tray, in use as a catchall for paint brushes and varnish, is a typical example.

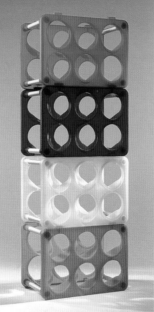

right Colorful plastic bottle crates brighten up a garage, cellar, modern kitchen, or understair area. Ideal for wine, water, or soft drinks, they can be stacked to save space. (Jasper Morrison rack.)

above For household maintenance or professional cleaning, this mobile unit offers a trash can and plastic vest for equipment. (From Slingsby.)

left Undersink pull-out plastic storage containers for household waste make recycling a practical option. Each one is split in half and lifts out separately for depositing in an outdoor recycling container, compost pile, or recycling bank. The lid lifts or seals automatically when the unit moves in or out. (Bin from Goldreif.)

below For outdoor use, this multipurpose container on wheels provides ample storage space for recycling papers, cans, or bottles. (Container from Slingsby.)

recycling

An active interest in recycling household waste requires specific storage. This can include a selection of individual or split bins with lids for every kind of waste product – from bottles and vegetable matter to paper and aluminum cans. If there is space under the sink or on the floor of a cabinet, a line of simple plastic buckets with lids will work as well as specialized storage items. Cardboard boxes from a supermarket are useful for storing newspapers.

directory

Check with the following suppliers and retailers for additional information about nationwide locations and/or mail order outlets.

UNITED STATES

Acme Display Fixture Co.
1057 South Olive Street
Los Angeles, CA 90015
tel 213-749-9191 or
800-959-5657

Ad Hoc Softwares
410 West Broadway
New York, NY 10012
tel 212-925-2652

Aero
132 Spring Street
New York, NY 10012
tel 212-966-1500

Bed & Bath & Beyond
620 Avenue of the Americas
New York, NY 10011
tel 212-255-3550

Bell 'Oggetti
711 Ginesi Drive
Morganville, NJ 07751
tel 800-644-3884

California Closet Co.
3385 Robertson Place
Los Angeles, CA 90034
tel 818-705-2300 or
800-274-6745 (for nearest
location)

C.I.T.E.
100 Wooster Street
New York, NY 10012
tel 212-431-7272
fax 212-226-6507

Clairson
International/Closetmaid
720 SW 17th Street
Ocala, FL 32674
tel 800-874-0008

Coconut Company
131 Greene Street
New York, NY 10012
tel 212-539-1940

Joan Cook
19 Foster Street
Peabody, MA 01961
tel 800-935-0971

Crate & Barrel
P. O. Box 9059
Wheeling, IL 60090
tel 800-323-5461 or
800-451-8217 (for nearest
location or catalog)

Dialogica
484 Broome Street
New York, NY 10013
tel 212-966-1934
fax 212-966-2870

Frank Eastern Co.
599 Broadway
New York, NY 10012
tel 212-219-0007

Elfa Marketing
2000 Valwood Parkway
Dallas, TX 75234
tel 800-394-3532

Equipto
225 Main Street
Tatamy, PA 18085
tel 800-323-0801

Fernlund & Logan
Architects
135 Rivington Street
New York, NY 10002
tel 212-473-7387
fax 212-674-9164

Tricia Foley
New York, NY
tel 212-348-0074
fax 212-423-9146

Gansevoort Gallery
72 Gansevoort Street
New York, NY 10014
tel 212-633-0555
fax 212-633-1808

Hirsh Company
8051 N. Central Park Avenue
Skokie, IL 60076
tel 847-673-6610

Hold Everything
P. O. Box 7807
San Francisco, CA 94120-7807
tel 800-421-2264 or
800-421-2285

Home Depot
499 Bobby Jones Expressway
Martinez, GA 30907
tel 706-650-7662 (for nearest
location)

Ikea
tel 800-434-4532 (for nearest
location or catalog)

Journeyman Products Ltd.
303 Najoles Road
Millersville, MD 21108
tel 800-248-8707

Kasten Inc.
5080 N. Ocean Drive
Slinger Island, FL 33404
tel 407-845-1087

Kate's Paperie
561 Broadway
New York, NY 10012
tel 800-809-9880

Lechters
tel 800-605-4824 (for nearest
location)

Lee/Rowan Company
900 Smith Highway Drive
Fenton, MO 63026
tel 800-325-6150

Ligne Roset (USA)
Corporation
New York Design Center
200 Lexington Avenue
Suite 601
New York, NY 10016
tel 212-685-2238

Modern Age
102 Wooster Street
New York, NY 10012
tel 212-966-0669
fax 212-966-4167

Modernica
7366 Beverly Boulevard
Los Angeles, CA 90036
tel 213-933-0383
fax 213-933-0159

National Business
Furniture, Inc.
735 Northwater Street
Milwaukee, WI 53202
tel 800-558-1010

Parallel Design
430 West 14th Street
Suite 408
New York, NY 10014
tel 212-989-4959
fax 212-989-4977

Pier One Imports
tel 800-447-4371 (for nearest
location)

Plexi-Craft Quality
Products Corp.
514 West 24th Street
New York, NY 10011
tel 212-924-3244

Pottery Barn
tel 800-922-5507 (for nearest
location)

Profiles
200 Lexington Avenue
New York, NY 10016
tel 212-689-6903

Rubbermaid
1147 Akron Road
Wooster, OH 44691
tel 216-264-6464

Rutt Custom Cabinetry
P. O. Box 129
Goodville, PA 17528
tel 215-445-6751

Schulte Corporation
12115 Ellington Court
Cincinnati, OH 45249
tel 800-669-3225

Annabelle Selldorf
Selldorf Architects
62 White Street
New York, NY 10013
tel 212-219-9571
fax 212-941-6362

The Shaker Shop
tel 800-834-8969

Smith & Hawken
Two Arbor Lane
Box 6900
Florence, KY 41022
tel 800-776-3336

Solutions
P.O. Box 6878
Portland, OR 97228
tel 800-342-9988

Staples
P.O. Box 1020
Westboro, MA 01581
*tel 800-333-3330 (for nearest
location)*

Waterworks
237 East 58th Street
New York, NY 10022
tel 212-371-9266

White Home Products
2401 Lake Park Drive
Atlanta, GA 30080
tel 800-431-0900

Windquest Company Inc.
3311 Windquest Drive
Holland, MI 49424
tel 800-562-4257

Vicente Wolf Associates
333 West 39th Street
New York, NY 10018
tel 212-465-0590
fax 212-465-0639

Zona
97 Greene Street
New York, NY 10012
tel 212 925 6750

OF SPECIAL NOTE

Stephen Mack
Stephen P. Mack Associates
Chase Hill Farm
Ashaway, RI 02804
tel 401-377-8041
*Stephen Mack is a nationally
renowned architectural and
interior designer and expert in
the restoration and reconstruction
of 17th- and 18th-century
structures and their environs.*

EUROPEAN EXPORT

The Conran Shop
Michelin House
81 Fulham Road
London WIP 9LH
England
tel 0171-636-9984

The Futon Company
169 Tottenham Court Road
London WIP 9LH
England
tel 0171-636-9984

H C Slingsby
(Head office and export)
Preston Street
Bradford BD7 1JF
tel 01274-721-591
fax 01274-723-044

**Arc Linea Arredamenti
Spa**
Via Pasubio 50
36030 Caldogno
Vicenza, Italy
tel 0444-39411
fax 0444-394262

Bieffeplast
Via Pelosa 78
35030 Caselle di Selvezzano
Padova, Italy
tel 0039-49 8730111
fax 0039-49 635323

Ligne Roset
95A High Street
Great Missenden
Buckinghamshire HP16 0AL
tel 01494-865001

**UK ARCHITECTS/
DESIGNERS**

*The following people can be
contacted for work outside of
the UK.*

Rick Baker
Workshop
F2 Cross Lane
London N8 7SA
England
tel 0181-340-2020
fax 0181-341-1620

Mark Gabbertas
Oblique Workshops
Stamford Works
Gillett Street
London N16 8JH
England
tel 0171-275-7495/
0171-381-1847

Nick Hill
85 Southbroom Road
Devizes
Wiltshire SN10 1LX
England
tel 01380-723-294

Janie Jackson
London, England
tel 0171-912-0882

Justin Meath Baker
Baker Nevile Associates
London, England
tel 0171-403-3137

Andrew Mortada
London, England
tel 0171-739-3027

**Munkenbeck + Marshall
Architects**
3 Pine Street
London, EC1R 0JH
England
tel 0171-833-1407
fax 0171-837-5416

Gunnar Orefelt
Orefelt Associates
4 Portobello Studios
5 Haydens Place
London, W11 1LY
England
tel 0171-243-3181
fax 0171-792-1126

Charles Rutherfoord
London, England
tel 0171-627-0182
fax 0171-720-0799

**Stickland Coombe
Architecture**
tel 0171-924-1699

Malcolm Temple
36 Trebovir Road
London SW5 9NJ
England
tel 0171-373-6122

projects

storage
boxes

Simple shoe boxes can make good-looking storage for home office items, such as notebooks and envelopes. This project explains how to cover and line a shoe box with identical fabric, although you can use remnants and mix and match different designs. Cotton, linen, or felt are ideal fabrics. If you have odds and ends of fabric, you can line the inside of the box with a different fabric than that used for the outside. Check that the shoe box is in good repair before you begin, and fasten down any internal flaps with glue, staples, or tape.

you will need:

⅓ yd (30 cm) of fabric

Shoe box

Pencil or tailor's chalk if the fabric is dark

Ruler, straight edge, or carpenter's square

Scissors

Cellophane tape, heavy book, or thumbtacks

Tape measure

Sheet of paper or newspaper

Rubber- or water-based glue (which will not stain or show through fabric; if you use felt, you can use double-sided tape instead of glue)

Hard rubber roller (optional)

Fray check (optional)

Ribbon or braid to decorate the outside of the lid (optional)

Label of some kind – possibly a photograph or plastic bag showing a sample of the box's contents (optional)

❶ Press the fabric flat with an iron and check that it is cut straight (at right angles) in the direction of the grain. Line up with the table, ruler, square, or shoe box to check. If necessary, you may have to trim the sides.

❷ Lay the fabric on a work table or cutting board. Using tape (or alternatively, a heavy book or thumbtacks), fix the fabric to the table so that it remains flat. Remove the lid from the shoe box and put it to one side.

❸ Cut two pieces of fabric: one piece of fabric will cover the outside base and ends (short sides) of the shoe box, inside and out; the other piece of fabric will cover the inside base and long sides of the shoe box, inside and out. You can use the shoe box to mark a template directly onto the fabric (see step 4). Alternatively, you can use a tape measure to measure the size of the box and mark the fabric, or make a pattern on a sheet of paper or newspaper and cut out the fabric the same size.

4 To measure the first piece, turn the shoe box on one side and line up the outside edges with the edges of fabric.

5 Mark the width of the box on the fabric with a pencil or chalk dot; flip the box along the fabric onto its base and opposite side. Use light dots to mark the outside points. This amount of fabric will cover the outside of the box.

6 To add enough fabric to line the two inside ends, move the box along the fabric to measure two more end pieces. Mark with pencil or chalk dots.

7 Now join all of the outer dots with a faint pencil or chalk line. Cut out the fabric. Attach this wide piece of fabric to the box first.

8 Apply a thin layer of glue on one outside long side of the box, and smooth the fabric over it. One end of the fabric should be in line with the base of the box.

9 Read the instructions on the glue – you may have to wait a while for the glue to dry. Now turn the box upright so that you can see into the shoe box. The fabric is going to line the inside of the box and the opposite outer side, so work with the bulk of the fabric toward you.

10 Apply glue to the first inner long side and smooth the fabric firmly, working from the middle of the cut edge of the fabric to the outside edges of the box and toward you. You may find that a rubber is useful. Wipe away excess glue if it oozes out from the sides, and take care not to get glue on the right side of the fabric.

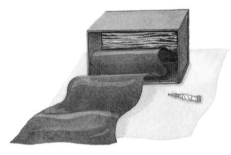

11 Apply glue to the base and second inner long side and smooth the fabric firmly. The fabric should fit neatly into the corners of the box. If you have cut more than you need, apply extra glue along the edges of the wrong side of the fabric and glue firmly to the box. Glue the last bit of fabric to the final outer long side, opposite the side where you began.

12 To cut the second piece of fabric, repeat the process but work along the length of the box instead of the width. Begin by turning the box on one end.

13 Glue the fabric to the inside end of the shoe box. Work around the outside of the box and the base, and finish on the opposite inside end.

14 Place the top of the lid face down on the fabric. Mark the size with pencil or chalk dots at each corner. Join the dots with a ruler and cut out. Unless you are using felt, apply fray check to the fabric edges before gluing.

15 Glue the fabric to the lid top, taking care to smooth all of the edges and corners. To finish the sides of the lid, cut a strip of fabric the length of all four sides (or use ribbon) and glue it to the lid.

16 For labeling, you could use index cards, luggage tags, or even a snapshot of what is inside. Better still, make your own visual index with sample contents in a transparent bag on the front of each box.

flatware
roll

A flatware roll is a traditional way to store precious silverware in individual pockets, free from dust and possible damage from scratching. Whether you have contemporary stainless steel flatware or more formal sterling silver, each roll makes a neat and easy package to store in a cabinet or drawer. It is also a convenient way to carry flatware to the table. If you have an extensive collection of sterling silver for big gatherings but use the same for everyday meals, store the bulk of the collection in individual rolls of knives and spoons and make a single roll for everyday place settings. If you want to keep all the pieces in circulation, switch the contents of the everyday roll from time to time. Alternatively, make individual flatware rolls for different members of the family — each one a different color.

you will need:

Soft dish towel or towel-sized piece of felt

Pins

Ruler

Pencil or tailor's chalk

Sewing machine or needle and thread

Approximately 24 in (60 cm) of tape or ribbon, or two 12-in. (30-cm) lengths

6 Stitch the outside seams and along the pencil lines or rows of pins with a good knot at the top of each of the seams. Remove the pins. (Baste and remove the pins for machine-stitching.)

1 Place the dish towel right side down and fold back approximately one-third of the length. Place an item of flatware on the fold-back to check that it is the right size to cover most of the handle. If you are mixing items in the same roll, check each piece for size on the fold-back. Expose enough of each handle to make the item easy to remove.

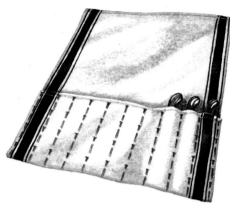

3 Continue along the roll, marking pockets with a line of pins. If you are mixing pieces in the same roll, measure each pocket with the relevant pieces; spoons need wider pockets than knives.

4 With identical items, save time by inserting an item, marking the width of the pocket, and marking the remaining pockets the same width with a ruler and pencil.

7 Insert the longest item of flatware and fold down the top of the towel to cover the pockets. Mark the fold line with a pin, remove the flatware, and press the top fold with an iron. This will help the top fold to lie flat on top of the flatware, hold its shape, and stay in place when rolled. For extra definition, machine-stitch a permanent crease along this fold.

2 Once you have established the correct size of the fold-back, pin it on both sides. Slip the piece of flatware inside the folded section of the towel, and pin along each side of the item to make a snug pocket.

5 Before you baste and stitch along each pencil line or row of pins, fold a length of ribbon in half lengthwise and insert the fold of the ribbon into one of the side seams near the top of the pockets. Because the ribbon will wrap around the roll to tie and secure the bundle, check that it will be on the outside edge when the towel is rolled. Insert the ribbon and pin in place.

hanging
rack

A soft hanging pocket is ideal for storing outdoor accessories like hats and scarves in hallways and porches. Make a storage rack by hanging a line of pockets beside or behind the front door on a length of dowel, a painted broom handle, or a bamboo pole suspended between two hooks. Hang two lines of pockets at different levels to suit different members of the family. Hanging pockets at child height is a friendly way to encourage children to store essential items of outdoor clothing in a convenient place – so they know where to find them!

you will need (for one pocket):

Fabric place mat

Pins

12 eyelets and eyelet tool

Woven fabric tape, approximately 1¼ in. (3 cm) wide or similar medium-density ribbon

Scissors

1 yd (1 m) of string or leather ribbon or cord

Sewing machine or needle and thread

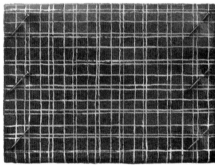

1 Fold the place mat in half, either lengthwise or widthwise depending on the shape of pocket you wish to make. Make three marks for eyelets along each side using pins. Position the pins evenly, approximately 32–40 in. (81–101 cm) apart, and pin front and back.

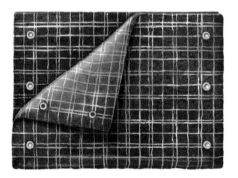

2 Now insert the eyelets (according to package directions) to correspond with the pin markers on each side of the fabric. Remove the pins.

3 Ribbons or cloth tape can be used to hang the pocket from a pole. Cut two identical strips; these will be attached to the top of the pocket.

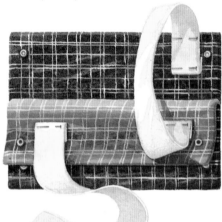

4 Make a loop with each strip on the inside of the pocket, as shown above. Pin in place, and tuck under the ends of tape for a neat finish. Machine- or hand-stitch.

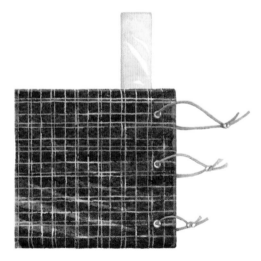

5 For built-in flexibility, tie the side seams with string or leather ribbon. Cut the string in varying lengths, so that the top piece is approximately twice as long as the bottom piece. Loop through the eyelets and knot.

underbed
storage

A low platform on wheels can create valuable extra storage by utilizing the space under the bed to store a wide range of items out of view. For magazines, spare bed linen, and sports shoes, use four 100 lb (45 kg) load-bearing castors, one in each corner, and a ½ in. (1.3 cm) depth platform. If you plan to store heavier items, check the load limit for each castor and use heavy-duty ones; choose a material with suitable strength and rigidity for the platform. Perhaps make two or three underbed platforms, accessible from different sides of the bed, and allocate to each platform a specific storage function such as camera equipment or household accounts. Store everyday items in frequent use at the front of the platform for easy access.

you will need:

Blockboard or wooden platform – ½ in. (1.3 cm) depth (Other dimensions are at your discretion – consider the size of bed and number of platforms.)

Pencil

Postcard or small piece of cardboard to improvise a square; or use a square or ruler

Castors (100 lb/45 kg) and screws

Drill

Screwdriver

Paint, tung oil, or varnish (if you plan to decorate or seal the platform)

"D" handle with hardware

❶ Place the platform surface upside down on a solid work table. (As an alternative work surface, protect a dining table with a spare blanket and newspapers.)

❷ To mark the position for one castor, square up a postcard in a corner of the platform, keeping the outside edges of the postcard in line with the outside edges of the platform. Draw a light pencil mark around the innermost corner of the postcard. Extend each pencil line by approximately 1½–2 in. (4–5 cm).

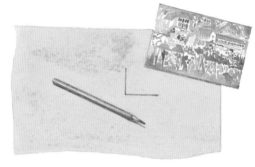

❸ Make pencil marks in this way in each corner. Use the pencil markings in each corner of the platform as a guide to position each castor.

❹ Set the castor right up against the pencil lines. Now mark the innermost screw position; drill a hole in the platform and position this screw.

❺ Double-check the alignment of the castor with the pencil lines, and mark the remaining screw positions. Drill and position the screws. Repeat for all castors.

❻ Turn the platform over again. If you plan to paint, seal, or varnish the wood, do so now – before you mount the handle in place. As an alternative to a "D" handle, you may want to make a rope pull. For this you need to drill two holes in the platform and thread thick rope through with a knot at each end on the underside.

❼ Mount the "D" handle on whichever end of the platform will be easiest to reach under the bed. For maximum flexibility and accessibility, you may want to place a handle on each side of the platform.

laundry
bag

A drawstring bag inside a laundry basket is ideal for concealing a mini-mountain of laundry – before or after washing. The bag folds down completely so that laundry can be stacked or sorted easily before it is concealed in the bag. It is useful for storing laundry, out-of-season clothes, spare blankets and pillows, or a mixture of items waiting for the next yard sale.

you will need:

A firm basket as base, ideally with handles on the side

2¾ yd (2.5 m) ticking or fabric (depending on size of basket)

Scissors

Pencil or tailor's chalk

Long ruler or straightedge

Pins

Sewing machine or needle and thread

10 feet (3 m) string or rope (depending on size of basket)

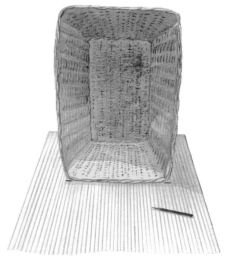

1 To make a bag, cut four pieces of fabric to fit inside the basket and extend approximately 20 in. (50 cm) beyond. First, lay the ticking wrong side up on a flat surface. You may want to fold the fabric in half so you can cut two side pieces and two end pieces at the same time. Next, turn the basket on one end. Position the basket on the fabric with enough room on each side to extend the diagonal lines of the basket by approximately 20 in. (50 cm). Mark the four outside corners of the basket with a pencil or chalk. Remove the basket and join the dots marked on the fabric with a straightedge across the bottom and along each side.

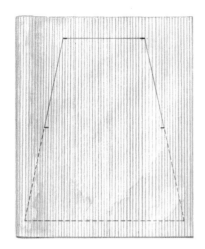

2 Following the diagonals of the sides of the basket, extend the side lines 20 in. (50 cm) beyond the top of the basket, or pencil markers. Join the marks across the top.

3 Now mark a cutting line ½ in. (1.3 cm) outside the first (sewing line) shape. Cut out. (If you cut without marking a cutting line, add a ½ in./1.3 cm seam allowance.)

4 Repeat steps 1–3 to cut out two more pieces for the sides of the basket. Stand the basket on its side and extend the diagonals by about 20 in. (50 cm), as before.

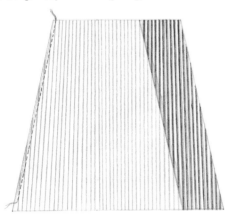

5 Still on the wrong side, pin, baste, and machine-stitch along the sewing lines, end to side piece, until all four pieces are sewn together. Stop 2½ in. (6 cm) below the top on every seam. This is the casing for the drawstring.

6 Now cut out a piece of fabric for the bottom of the basket. Stand the basket upright on the wrong side of the fabric. Mark all four corners with a pencil. Remove the basket and join the dots. This is a sewing line. Adding a ½ in. (1.3 cm) seam allowance, cut out the fabric.

7 Line up the bottom sides of the bag with the sides of the base fabric, right sides together. Pin, baste, and sew together each long side to the end of each sewing line.

8 After the sides are complete, repeat step 7 to join the ends to the bottom.

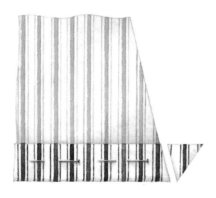

9 To make a casing for the drawstring at the top of the bag, tuck under the cut edge of the fabric for a neat finish and turn back on the inside of the bag approximately 1 in. (2.5 cm). Pin in place. Trim the excess fabric corners in line with the diagonal sides of the bag.

10 Sew the casing seam by hand and remove the pins or, if machine-stitching, baste the seams and remove the pins before sewing. At each corner, tuck in each cut end of fabric and sew in place, taking care to leave an opening for the string or rope to pass through.

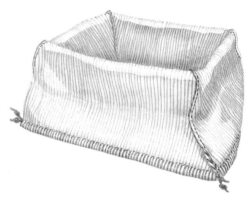

11 Cut two lengths of string or rope for the sides. Make the lengths as long as the sides, plus enough to make a substantial knot at each end. Cut two lengths of string for the ends in the same way. Knot one end of the string, thread the other end through the relevant side or end of the bag, and then knot the remaining end. (If you have difficulty threading the string through the channels, attach the end of the string to a safety pin and push the pin through.) Using four lengths of string allows each panel to be opened and closed individually.

tool
holder

This carry-all means that small garden tools, twine, and seed packs are within easy reach for simple gardening chores. It can be tied to a garden bucket or the front of a wheel-barrow between the handles, or even worn around the waist. Made from plastic-coated cotton, it is easy to wipe clean, and hook-and-loop-tape seams open out flat so you can get rid of any lingering soil or stray seed.

you will need:

18 x 26 in. (45 x 66 cm) plastic-coated cotton or medium-weight vinyl

Double-sided tape

Scissors

Approx. 12 self-adhesive hook-and-loop dots

Approx. 2 yd (2 m) string, cut in half

Large safety pin (optional)

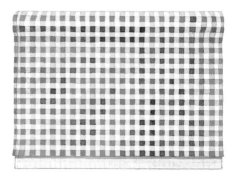

1 Lay the length of fabric right side down on a work surface. Fold the fabric down almost in half lengthwise, leaving about ¾ in. (2 cm) of reverse fabric showing.

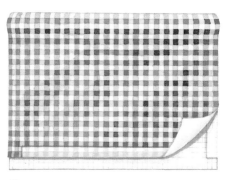

2 Put double-sided tape along the bottom width of the uppermost face and along each inside edge, stopping approximately ¾ in. (2 cm) short of the top fold.

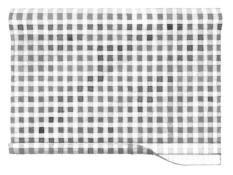

3 Peel off the protective strip and seal the fabric on both sides. Fold up the bottom section and press firmly onto the uppermost face to seal the fabric on all three sides.

4 Position garden tools on top of the sealed fabric with the handles extending beyond the top fold. Turn up the bottom half of the fabric to ¾ in. (2 cm) short of the fold. Pin through the top layer only to mark seams between each tool. Mark the line of the bottom fold and the position of the top flap, ¾ in. (2 cm) short of the top fold.

5 Remove the tools and open out the fabric. Divide and stick six pairs of hook-and-loop dots along each vertical seam, including outside edges, taking care to marry positive and negative dots.

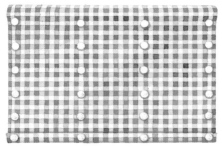

6 Now fold the fabric along the line of pin markers, align the hook-and-loop dots, press firmly, and remove pins. To tie the tool holder to a bucket or wheelbarrow, loop the two lengths of string, each about 1 yd (1 m) long, to thread through the top fold of fabric. If the tool bag is to be worn around your waist, tie a length of string loosely around your waist to find the correct length, cut another identical length and loop the two lengths together.

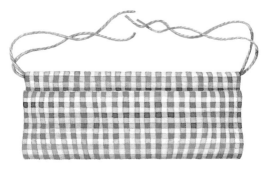

7 Thread two ends of the same piece of string through the top fold of the fabric so that the loop sits in the middle of the fold. If this is difficult, attach the two ends of string to a large safety pin and push it through. Tie the tool holder to a bucket or wheelbarrow and lightly gather the fabric over the string so that the pockets do not lie completely flat.

shower **curtain**

This is an inventive and practical way to store everything you need for a shower. Shampoo, sponges, brushes, and shower gel fit into convenient pockets that line down the inside of a shower curtain. Items can be left in the pockets after you have finished showering. Stack personal toiletries at a handy level for individual members of the family – child-friendly shampoos and gels can be placed within easy reach for children; teenage lotions and potions somewhere in the middle; and adult oils and specialty products at the top. The pockets are angled for easy access, storage, and effective drainage, and open stitching means that any water in the pockets will drain down into the shower stall or bathtub. If you are using thin plastic shower curtains, do not overload them because they may tear with the weight of the items. Alternatively, for extra strength, use a plastic-coated fabric shower curtain.

you will need:

Shower curtain and rings

Dressmaking pins

Chalk (or dressmaker's pencil)

Ruler

Heavy-duty nylon thread or fishing line

Needle with a large eye

Scissors

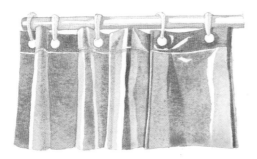

1 Hang up the shower curtain and double up the last two hooks, turning the end in toward the shower to create the pocket flap.

2 Consider what items you want to store in the pockets and where. As a guide, line up on the floor any bottles and sponges you use every time you have a shower. Position items according to the heights of family members.

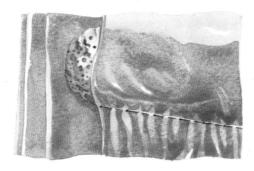

3 Working from the top of the curtain, mark the seam for the first pocket. Push dressmaking pins through the double thickness of the folded shower curtain. Begin at the turned-in edge and make a gradual diagonal line down toward the fold. Insert the uppermost bottle or accessory and leave it in place.

4 Slide the second bottle or accessory into place below the first pocket. Check that there is enough room for easy access. Mark the position of this item with a pin for the second seam, and put the bottle or accessory to one side. Pin a diagonal line to mark the second seam, as before, and put the bottle or accessory back in place.

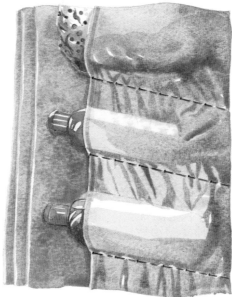

5 Continue down the shower curtain, marking pockets for items. Leave everything in place as you work and be careful not to overload the fabric. Thin plastic shower curtains will hang out of shape and may tear if overloaded.

6 Empty the pockets. If you feel confident sewing the shower curtain while it is hanging without a pencil line as a guide, leave it hanging and ignore the next step. Otherwise, take down the shower curtain and move to a work table.

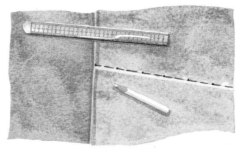

7 To guide the stitching, assess stitch sizes, and make a neat diagonal, use a ruler and chalk marker at this stage. Place the ruler just under the line of pins. Using the chalk marker, make ¾-in. (2-cm) dashes along the ruler. This broken line will be a guideline for a running stitch. A ¾-in. (2-cm) stitch length is ideal to allow easy drainage.

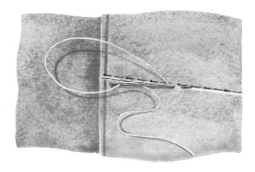

8 Leave the dressmaking pins in place. Now, using nylon thread, begin sewing from the opening of the pocket, securing the end of the nylon thread with a good knot. Stitch along the pencil line and knot again at the fold. Use transparent or white nylon thread for a simple style, or use a color if you want a decorative contrast.

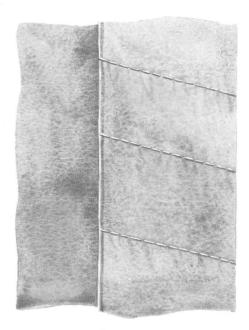

9 Continue down, sewing all of the seams in this way, leaving the pins in place until you have sewn each seam. Once each seam has been sewn, remove the pins.

vegetable rack

This hanging vegetable rack is a practical way to divide and store fresh vegetables. Its multitiered construction means it is easy to see which vegetables you have on hand, and it can be dismantled for cleaning. The holes in the colanders allow air to circulate around the vegetables and help maintain their freshness, so this design is good for storing root vegetables (such as potatoes, onions, and turnips) and fruit. The colanders used here are medium size, which limits the vegetables to an appropriate weight for the chain and hooks. If you want to increase the size of colander and storage capacity, simply use heavier chains and hooks and secure a firm fixture to the ceiling or kitchen rack.

you will need:

As many colanders (metal or plastic) as you want for your rack – each 9½ in. (24 cm) diameter

"S" hook

Hook to attach vegetable rack to ceiling (or butcher's hook to hang it from kitchen rack)

Bolt cutter to cut chain

Pliers and pinchers to open chain

For every colander:

2 spring hooks

Approximately 1 yd (1 m) of chain. (Take exact measurements when you buy the chain – you may be able to get it cut to length by the supplier.)

1 Measure the distance from the ceiling or kitchen rack to where you want the first colander to hang. Cut two lengths of chain this length and join the pieces at the top with the "S" hook. This hook can loop onto a ceiling hook or butcher's hook suspended on a kitchen rack.

3 To hang the second colander, hold it below the first in position, and measure the distance between the two. At this stage you will find it easier to position additional colanders if you hang up the first. If you are not ready to hang the vegetable rack in its place in the kitchen, hang it on a clothesline or on a hanger in the closet so you can continue working on it.

2 Connect the other ends of the two lengths of chain to the handles of the colander with spring hooks.

4 You will now need to cut two more lengths of chain, to the measurements determined in step 3 above. Attach each end of chain to the spring hooks on the first colander.

5 To create the second tier of your vegetable rack, connect the ends of the chain to the handles of the second colander with spring hooks.

6 Your vegetable rack is now complete. If you require more storage, you can add one or two more colanders with chains and spring hooks.

Alternative: Instead of measuring and cutting chains yourself, you can use ready-made kits for outdoor hanging baskets. Such kits supply three chains for every basket, whereas this technique requires two chains — so remove one of the chains with pliers and pinchers or a bolt cutter.

roller **bin**

Anything from magazines and books to lap-top hobbies like knitting or Nintendo can all be stored neatly and conveniently in a personalized roller bin. Wheel the bin alongside your chair when you put your feet up and store it out of the way behind the sofa or under the television table when it is not in use. Choose a bin that fits in with your interior decoration.

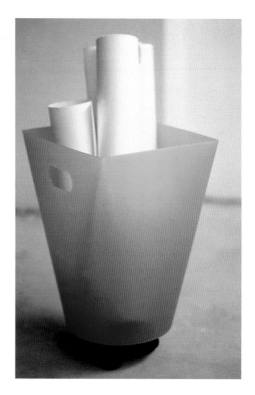

you will need:

Bin

2 cake boards (available in cooking or baking stores) or 2 pieces of corrugated cardboard or chipboard (square or round to fit into the bottom of the bin)

Glue (appropriate to the type of bin)

Drill

2 nuts and bolts with washers

4 castors with screws (same depth as 1 cake board)

Screwdriver

1 Turn the bin upside down and glue a cake board to the bottom. Follow the glue manufacturers' instructions.

2 Turn the bin so that it is upright again, and mount the second cake board inside in exactly the same position as the first. Stand a weight inside the bin on the board – a book, for example – and allow the glue to dry.

3 When the glue is dry, secure the new base by drilling two holes through both of the cake boards and through the bottom of the bin. When drilling, place the bin half on and half off the end of a table – or a step. Drill through the side half off the table or step first and then rotate the bin and drill a hole in the opposite side.

4 Secure the base by inserting two nuts and bolts through these holes – through both cake boards and the bottom of the bin. Position the nuts on the outside of the bin.

5 When the cake boards are firmly attached to each other and the bin, mount the castors on the outside cake board only. Position each castor evenly around the outside edge of the cake board and draw around each castor fixture. Working on one castor at time, mark one screw hole and screw it in, taking care that the screw is the right size to penetrate the outer cake board only. Realign the castor if necessary, mark the remaining screw holes, and screw it in. Repeat for the remaining three castors.

basics

kitchen
planning

There is no set plan for designing a perfect kitchen. Begin by assessing your requirements for equipment and storage (i.e. do six people sit down at the kitchen table every day, or two people once a week?); and take into account existing architecture. Choose a practical plan to maximize space and create a welcoming environment.

Beginning with simple ergonomics, position key activity areas within an imaginary compact triangle – kitchen sink, cooking facilities, and refrigerator. Provide ample work surfaces in between or adjacent to each area and incorporate no-fuss storage for equipment, cookware, and tableware within easy reach. Store pots and pans next to cooking facilities, and knives and chopping boards next to a food preparation surface. Install good lighting throughout, paying special attention to high-visibility cooking and work surfaces.

The illustration opposite of a single-line kitchen extends along a 3⅓-yard (3-meter) wall and contains the essential elements. Use this as a guide to ergonomics and general planning. For anyone with a disability or mobility restriction, consult your local consumer advice office or relevant charity for specialist advice.

1 An industrial-style stainless steel cart with shelves is a versatile addition to a busy or compact kitchen. Incorporate a permanent space underneath a work surface to store the cart when not in use and maintain a clear thoroughfare.

2 The top shelf of a cart provides a useful "backup" work surface, or storage space for pans or cookware. Alternatively, fit the cart with a good-size chopping board or piece of marble for food preparation.

3 Secondary shelves on carts provide permanent storage for pots, pans, and cookware. Wheel it out next to a cooking area for easy access or line it up alongside a work surface to make a practical L-shape.

4 Leave everyday electrical appliances like toasters on display on a work surface or convenient solid shelf for easy access. Position them next to an existing or new electrical outlet and trim cords, or, if possible, rewind onto the appliance to cut down on excessive visible wiring.

5 Inserting a burner in a work surface with a separate single oven below is space-efficient and offers flexibility to mix and match gas and electrical appliances according to personal preference. This arrangement leaves enough space below the oven for an expansive drawer for baking trays, large pans, or chopping boards.

6 Store kitchen knives, flatware, and utensils in a slim-line set of drawers with everyday items in the top drawers for convenience and specialized items below. In standard-size drawers fit dividers or lift-out plastic trays and keep knives and utensils in separate compartments.

7 An open metal or wooden shelf on wall brackets can store cooking oils, everyday food items, and spice jars – all within easy reach of a cooking or food preparation surface. It is also convenient for stacks of plates, cups, and glasses.

8 Decorative and functional, hanging storage for saucepans and stainless steel utensils provides direct access to everyday equipment for busy cooks, and keeps work surfaces free for food preparation. Suspend a metal rod with secure wall hardware every 30 inches (76.2 cm)— every 20 inches (50.8 cm) to support cast iron or copper pans—with an array of butchers' hooks.

9 Leave a section of a hanging rail free for dish towels and oven mitts.

10 Areas next to sinks and stoves are key food preparation surfaces. In a compact kitchen line-up, incorporate a large work surface and keep it free from electrical appliances or clutter. If space is too tight for an adequate work surface, install burners with a lid to double as a work surface and set a wooden board over the sink. Alternatively, mount a retractable board under a work surface or keep a simple folding table or cart on hand.

11 To match the style of surrounding kitchen cabinets or fixtures, fix a fascia or decor panel to appliance doors, or install an appliance inside a standard frame and remove the back for ventilation or plumbing. All appliances fit underneath a standard 36-inch (91.4-cm) work surface, apart from mini appliances. If you need a work surface at a different height, mount an independent work surface with wall battens and brackets or stand it on metal or wooden legs. Do not sit an independent work surface on top of cabinets without any mountings, as this will not be stable.

12 Store a flip-top bin out of the way under a sink. It is convenient for vegetable trimmings or peelings and for throwing away waste food before rinsing plates.

13 For an inexpensive recycling system, use a selection of mini plastic bins or buckets for bottles, aluminum cans, and paper. Alternatively, use specialized recycling bins with individual compartments for waste products, or use a large bin with several different sacks or shopping bags inside.

14 Store basic cleaning equipment and buckets in an undersink cabinet. Use any extra space above the bucket to fix a simple shelf for storing cloths, brushes, and sponges. Or hang the bucket on a hook on the side of the cabinet for extra cleaning equipment.

1 Storage space for cart

2 Cart with work surface

3 Shelf for bowls and cookware

4 Work surface for small electrical appliances, etc.

5 Oven with drawer below for baking sheets, etc.

6 Drawer system for flatware, knives, and utensils

7 Open shelf for oils, spice jars, and everyday food items

8 Steel or wooden pole with butchers' hooks

9 Storage space for dish towels and oven mitts

10 Work surface for food preparation

11 Fridge with fascia panel in keeping with cabinets

12 Undersink flip-top bin for kitchen waste

13 Individual plastic buckets for recycling bottles and cans

14 Cleaning bucket and equipment

closet
planning

The illustration opposite shows a one-wall flexible storage system for clothing – easily adaptable to fit individual needs. To assess individual requirements, write an inventory of clothing, and anything else you want to store (such as sports equipment). Alternatively, lay out items of clothing and divide them into piles as a guide to how much hanging space and how many shelves to allocate. Incorporate extra space for new acquisitions and add an extra one-quarter of the total storage space to accommodate this.

Organization and flexibility inside a closet are the key to workable clothing storage. Use ready-made units or modular systems with optional fill-ins for a practical arrangement of hanging rods, shelves, and drawers. Alternatively, put together an inexpensive system using vertical tracks and adjustable shelves, hanging rods, and a self-assembly set of drawers. Once you have established the basics, hang doors, sliding panels, or shades or drapes on a curtain pole.

Use this general guide to measurements when planning space-efficient storage, although you should always check measurements of specific items and, if mixing different sizes of clothing, base measurements on largest jackets and shoe sizes.

1 Store seasonal items such as suitcases, sports racquets, or spare blankets on top shelves. Leave this space open for maximum flexibility. As a safety precaution, avoid storing heavy items or boxes out of reach on high shelves.

2 Store shoes in boxes to help maintain their shape and protect from dust and scratches. Use white or unbleached tissue paper to stuff toes, and wrap suede, patent leather, or special-finish shoes individually or use plastic or cedar shoe trees. For quick access, store shoes either without boxes on shelves, on slanting shoe racks underneath hanging clothing, or in canvas shoe organizers inside closet doors. Loosely knot together laces of sports shoes and canvas pumps and loop over simple hooks.

3 Fold and pack clean out-of-season clothing in large cardboard boxes with lids, and stand boxes on the floor or base of a closet. To prevent possible discoloration or damage, do not stand these boxes next to a heating pipe or radiator. Layer each box, placing heavy items (jackets, coats, or woolens) on the bottom and lightweight items (shirts and T-shirts) on top. Use tissue paper to interline and protect delicate or special items or fold carefully inside a plain white cotton or linen pillowcase.

4 Separate individual hats with plain tissue paper and store several in a box to maintain shape and protect from dust, light, and moth damage.

5 Store bags and briefcases, including sport sacks and overnight bags, in shelves with upright dividers. Snap or zip all bags shut and stuff leather or satin with tissue paper to maintain good shape.

6 Install a hanging rod in a space 24 inches (61 cm) wide for coats and dresses – allow 1½–3 inches (3.8–7.6 cm) of rail for every item and a 60-inch (152.4-cm) drop. This drop will not accommodate floor-length dresses and coats, so either pack these in tissue paper and boxes, loop them across two coat hangers, or measure individual items and allocate more hanging space. Alternatively, divide a hanging space with a vertical wooden panel or post and set rods at different heights. Use brass rods for maximum weight

capacity and support every 40 inches (101.6 cm). To protect items from dust or possible discoloration, store them in canvas clothing bags with a transparent front to identify contents. To prevent possible moth damage for everyday clothing, hang odorfree moth deterrents or cedar balls so that air can circulate and they don't contact any items of clothing.

7 Jackets and shirts need 40 inches (101.6 cm) of hanging space. Allow approximately 1½–3 inches (3.8–7.6 cm) of rail space for each shirt, 1½–2⅛ inches (3.8–5.4 cm) for a cotton or linen jacket and 2⅛–3 inches (5.4–7.6 cm) for a wool jacket. Wire hangers are ideal for cotton shirts. Use satin or cotton padded hangers for linens, silks, and woolens, or cover wire hangers with tissue paper to avoid marking fabric. Include a round hanger for neckties and belts or hang them on hooks inside the closet door.

8 Allow 40 inches (101.6 cm) of hanging space for slacks, skirts, and separates and 1½ inches (3.8 cm) of rod space for every item, depending on materials.

9 Use drawers to store underwear, socks, belts, and scarves. For extra organization, insert drawer dividers and store pairs of socks or hose in separate compartments ranging in colors from light to dark.

10 Store rarely used items in spare boxes on top shelves. Line airtight boxes with felt for dress jewelry and beads. Store precious items in individual felt or brushed cotton drawstring bags or mini-safes.

11 Lie shawls, throws, and fake-fur wraps in loose folds on a wide open shelf. Alternatively, use this space for extra pillows, sport equipment, or luggage.

12 For easy access, divide sweaters and shirts into different colors and stack three or four items in open shelves or boxes. For extra protection from dust or for delicate items, use plastic or canvas storage envelopes.

13 Store jeans, T-shirts, and casual clothing in open shelves or boxes and fold or roll to avoid creasing.

1 Open shelf or space for luggage

2 Open shelving for shoe boxes or shoe bags

3 Storage boxes with lids for out-of-season clothing

4 Hat boxes

5 Bags in individual upright slots

6 Hanging rod for long dresses and coats

7 Hanging rod for jackets and shirts

8 Hanging rod for separates, skirts, and slacks

9 Drawers for underwear, T-shirts, belts, and scarves

10 Open shelf for extra storage boxes or spare blankets

11 Open shelf for throws, scarves, and shawls

12 Open boxes for shirts and sweaters in envelopes

13 Open boxes for jeans, T-shirts, and casual clothing

creating
storage

Mounting brackets

As a rough guide to choosing a bracket, find one that will support three-quarters of the width of the shelf. Brackets should be set approximately every 30 inches (76.2 cm) along the length, although this measurement will differ depending upon the materials that you use for the shelf and what you plan to store or display. For example, solid wooden shelves with a depth of ¾ inch (1.9 cm) require a support bracket every 18 inches (45.7 cm). For formica or blockboard shelving use a minimum ½ inch (1.3 cm) shelf depth or fix a wooden facing to the front of the shelves to prevent bowing.

The key to a secure shelf is a good anchor on the wall. If you change the use of the shelf, review the position of the brackets. For example, if you put up a kitchen shelf to store glasses and later decide to stack plates or saucepans instead, add more brackets to compensate for the increase in load.

Measure the shelf and figure out an even spacing for the brackets. If you plan to use part of the shelf for stereo equipment, part for CDs, and part for ceramics or artifacts, divide the shelf into sections and space the brackets evenly within each section – with less space between brackets for the hi-fi section and more space between brackets for the CD section. Make a note of any measurements and check that they all add up to the shelf length before you begin drilling the holes. Always check the construction of the wall before putting up your shelves – some walls are not loadbearing.

1 If you know exactly where you want a shelf, you can start measuring immediately. Or position the shelf by measuring from the floor. Alternatively, hold the shelf in place and make a faint pencil mark on the wall directly under the shelf. Put the shelf to one side.

2 To mount the first bracket, line up the top of the bracket with the shelf pencil mark. Make a pencil mark through the uppermost hole on the wall-mounting part of the bracket. Put the bracket to one side, drill a hole on the pencil mark, insert an anchor and screw the bracket in place, allowing a little "give" for repositioning. Use a level on top of the bracket, and make adjustments before marking the subsequent points for the wall mounting.

3 Depending on the design of the bracket, you may be able to tighten the first screw and leave the bracket in place for the others. Alternatively, slide the bracket to one side, drill the holes, and tighten all the screws when all hardware is in place, after a final check with a level.

4 Mount all remaining brackets. Either lay the level on top of the first bracket and support the other end

with the second bracket, or hold the shelf in place with the level sitting on top and mark the position for the second bracket this way.

5 Mark and install one bracket at a time. Once all the brackets have been secured to the wall, put the shelf in place and, using a pencil, mark the position for the screws through the shelf-mount part of the brackets. If you want to make holes in the shelf for electric cords, mark the position for these also.

6 Remove the shelf and drill holes on the pencil marks for the shelf hardware, taking care not to drill through the shelf. Drill any other holes for electric cords. Replace the shelf and secure.

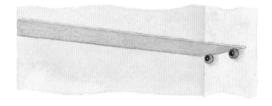

Alternative shelving

A glass shelf with four rubber doorstops in each corner instead of brackets provides an alternative to traditional shelving. Set in alcoves, approximately 30 inches (76.2 cm) wide, with the rubber stops as supports on side walls, the shelf is ideal storage for a range of small-scale items including CDs, books, or medium-weight artifacts. Use strengthened (or minimum ¼ inch/.64 cm-thick) glass, and drill bits and wall plugs that are appropriate for the specific type of masonry or wall – for example, plaster board. Screws should be three times as long as the rubber stop – two-thirds of the length of the screw for internal anchorage and one-third to hold the rubber stop in place.

1 Hold the shelf in place and mark a pencil dot on the back of the side wall underneath the shelf – approximately one-fifth of the width of the shelf away from the back edge of the shelf.

2 To anchor the first rubber stop, put the shelf down and line up the center-top of the stop with the pencil dot. Push the pencil through the middle of the rubber stop and mark the wall for the first drill hole. Drill the hole, insert an anchor, and screw the rubber stop in place.

3 To anchor the second rubber stop on the same wall, hold the glass shelf in place resting on the first rubber stop and place a level on the glass across its width. Check the level and mark a pencil dot on the wall underneath the shelf one-fifth of the width away from the front outside edge of the shelf.

4 Put the glass to one side and proceed as before. Line up the center-top of the rubber stop with the pencil dot, push the pencil through the middle of the rubber stop, and mark for drilling. After each fixing, hold the shelf in place, check that it is level (using a level), and make the next mark.

5 Put nonslip adhesive pads on the underside of the glass in line with the rubber stops to prevent the shelf from slipping, and slot the shelf in place.

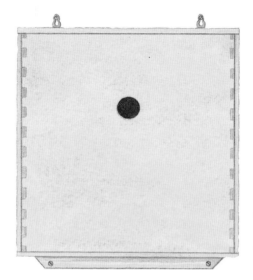

Mirror plates

For use in supporting and positioning traditional wall cupboards, mirror plates hook onto screws or nails in a wall. As extra support, you can put wooden battens on the wall under the unit to take weight off the mirror plates. The batten can be as long as the cabinet or, for a less obtrusive effect, fix two short battens. Usually mirror plates are unseen; either the top of the cupboard or shelf is above eye level or items on the shelf conceal the fixtures. However, if the mirror plates are on view and you want to disguise the brass finish and wall screw, apply an undercoat suitable for metal finishes and then paint it the same color as the wall. Protect the cabinet or shelf with masking tape when you paint, or paint the mirror plate before you mount it.

To mount a storage box with pull-out drawer on the wall with mirror plates:

1 Work on the back of the box. Measure a quarter of the length in from each side and make pencil marks. This is where you will set the mirror plates.

2 Position one brass mirror plate over a pencil mark so that the top of the mirror plate to be mounted on the wall is above the top of the box. Push the pencil through each screw hole on the part of the mirror plate to be mounted on the box and make marks. It may be possible to screw directly into the wood without drilling first. Put both the mirror plates on the box.

3 Hold the box against the wall and place a level on top. When the box is in position, make pencil marks through the uppermost hole in the mirror plate (the plate slides down the wall fixture to rest at this point). Mount one screw on the wall, leaving enough of the screw head unscrewed to allow the mirror plate to slide behind. (You can tighten each screw onto the mirror plate at the end to make sure that it is secure.) Hang the box on one screw, supporting the opposite side. Place a level on top, and check the mark for the second screw before screwing.

4 If you plan to mount battens on the wall for extra support, hang the box and make pencil marks directly underneath in line with each mirror plate. Put the box down. Use the marks to position a single batten or two smaller battens. Line up the top of the battens with the marks, and drill through each end of the battens into the wall. Insert anchors in the wall and mount the battens in place with screws. Alternatively, line up the top of the battens with the pencil marks, mark directly underneath again, and put the battens to one side. Drill into the wall directly in the middle of the pencil marks on each end of the battens, and insert plugs. Drill identical holes through the battens, measure to check the position, then screw it in place.

5 Rehang the box. Drop the box gently onto the battens and tighten the screws on the mirror plates. If you are hanging a shelf this way with a batten underneath, you can screw down through the back of the shelf into the batten. Be careful to avoid the wall hardware.

safety and storage
advice

When contemplating your storage options, it is important to bear in mind basic safety points and practical elements. An extensive checklist follows, which includes general advice and safety precautions for each area of your home.

Also included is safety advice if you are planning to undertake any do-it-yourself home projects, or moving or assembling furniture. Over and above specific instructions supplied by the manufacturer, always follow the measures on page 169.

Kitchens

● Store cleaning equipment and chemicals out of reach of children. If you choose to store cleaning equipment in an undersink cupboard, always install a lock or safety catch on the door.

● Keep a fire extinguisher in an accessible place in the kitchen in the event of a pan or cooking fire.

● Never hang dish towels or cloths from butchers' hooks or hanging rods above stoves or cooking facilities, to avoid any risk of fire.

● Do not install stoves or cooking facilities next to shades or curtains. This can present a fire risk.

● To avoid any risk of fire, do not install wall cabinets or shelves above stoves or cooking facilities.

● Stacks of china should be stored on open shelves in single stacks for convenience and to avoid overloading – for example, keep stacks of plates, cereal bowls, and saucers separate on a shelf. Always dry crockery thoroughly before stacking it.

● When storing precious china, wrap each item individually in fabric sleeves or insert a sheet of corrugated paper or cotton batting between each plate.

● Sterling silver is easily tarnished by light, damp, and acid in wood. Store silverware in a roll. Alternatively, use a length of felt and lay a piece at one end, roll and cover, insert another piece and continue until all the pieces are bound together. Tie the bundle with ribbon or string to keep it intact.

● Do not mix sterling silver and stainless flatware in the same tray. Contact with stainless steel will invariably damage silver over time. They should also be separated in the dishwasher.

● Water and electricity do not mix—to avoid splashing and the risk of damage to the electrical system or worse, electrocution, do not position electrical outlets next to a sink or water supply.

● Avoid cabinet doors opening outward into a kitchen and blocking a thoroughfare. Use two doors instead of one, a sliding panel, or a shutter – or move the cabinet.

● Pay special attention to the position of dishwashers and beware of dishwasher doors obstructing or restricting movement around the kitchen.

● Shelves installed above eye level are suitable for lightweight, rarely used items only. Use a step ladder to remove anything. Do not attempt to remove any item you cannot see and never pull on a shelf for support.

● To stabilize carts, especially if you are using a cart as an extra work surface beside a cooking facility, set wheel brakes on opposite sides of the base.

● Always store knives, scissors, and any hazardous utensils or electrical equipment out of reach of children.

● Check ventilation requirements before installing any electrical appliance, especially if you plan to conceal them. If in any doubt, call in a registered professional or contact the manufacturer for expert advice.

● Do not attempt to connect a gas appliance yourself. Contact a registered professional or your local gas board.

● Leave irons standing upright to cool before putting them away in a cabinet, to avoid any risk of fire.

● Allow adequate space between a work surface and wall cabinet. If space is at a premium, consider installing open shelves instead of cabinets to avoid the hazard of doors opening at head height in a compact environment.

● To avoid steam and heat damage (and a possible fire hazard), do not place coffee makers and toasters directly underneath wooden shelving.

Bathrooms

● Always store medicines out of reach of children. Either use a specialized medicine chest with a lock or safety catch, or secure a conventional cabinet.

● Keep razors, scissors, tweezers, and any chemicals or hazardous lotions out of reach of children – preferably in locked wall cabinets.

● Store bleach or cleaning equipment out of reach of children, under lock and key.

Living areas

● Entertainment equipment requires full support on secure shelving with adequate allowance for cords and connections behind. (Install narrower shelves above for books and artifacts.)

● Do not overload electrical outlets. Bind together or cover electrical cables to avoid any risk of entanglement or tripping. Look for plastic sheathing that groups cables safely or specialized stereo shelving systems with hollow vertical supports to conceal cables. Alternatively, drill holes through the backs of units and cupboards, and tape or anchor cords/cables to shelves, supports, and along baseboards.

● Do not position cabinets directly in front of outlets; this obstructs access and can present a hazard.

● If you use a cart to store entertainment equipment, always disconnect the electrical supply before moving the cart. (If you forget, the plug will remain in the socket and your TV or VCR will end up on the floor.)

● Avoid overloading shelves with books, equipment, or collectibles, and store heavy items on bottom shelves.

● Screw or bolt freestanding cabinets to a wall or insert wedges at the base to make sure that the cabinet cannot tip forward. (A wall cabinet is a climbing temptation to young children.)

● Store photographs in albums, acid-free plastic envelopes, or archive boxes and use photographic mounts; ordinary papers and glues will damage prints over time. Display valuable photographic prints in frames to protect from dust and keep out of direct sunlight to prevent fading, or use nonreflective glass. Negatives require specialized storage in acid-free files. Keep an index for efficiency and time-saving.

● To protect glass shelves from scratches, use felt pads or cotton mats (on metal feet of stereo equipment, wooden or metal artifacts, sculptures, or collections of pebbles, for example).

● If you have young children, avoid random stacks of any kind of storage boxes as these can be easily knocked over. Place them safely into an open shelf system instead.

General

● If valuable items are to be stored in an attic or basement, always check for leaks and dampness beforehand.

● Keep computer equipment in a cool, dry place and away from direct sunlight and smoky atmospheres.

● Store floppy disks for computers in custom-designed boxes to prevent them from being damaged.

Advice for home projects

● Dress for protection when embarking on any handyman project. Ideally, you should wear overalls. In some cases, you may need to wear protective gloves, goggles, or a mask.

● Plan each project carefully and check that you have all the necessary tools and equipment before you begin.

● Read all the instructions for self-assembly kit furniture and keep screws and fixtures safe and at hand in a bowl or plastic bag. File instructions for future reference. Do not attempt to assemble a large item alone, and assemble things *in situ* if you can.

● Store tools in a dry cupboard or shed to prevent rust, and keep out of reach of children. Store paint, varnish, and any chemicals in well-sealed, upright cans.

● When installing shelves or cabinets, always use the relevant screws, wall plugs, and drill bits. For solid walls, use masonry drill attachments and hardware. For stud or hollow walls, use either wooden fixtures for wooden studs or cavity fixtures for wallboard in between, depending on load capacity. Check with individual suppliers for specific product information and load capacity.

credits

Products featured in this book are available from the following manufacturers and suppliers. For full contact details, see the directory (pages 141–44).

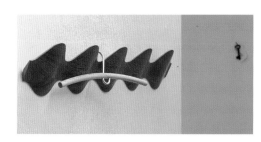

pages 42–43
Low table in oak designed by Maarten Van Severen, Viaduct; Franchi shelving system with adjustable shelves in birch ply and Tall Boy drawers in MDF with leather pulls, Mark Gabbertas; three-tier Klein cupboard, Jinan Furniture Gallery.

pages 108–9
Double laundry bin in plywood and laundry tub, The Conran Shop; Bubu stool by Philippe Starck, Purves and Purves.

pages 62–63
Peep nightstand, The Conran Shop; Nazanin Kamali bedroom storage cabinet, Aero; Flow chest of drawers and Ebb nightstand in ash or cherry veneer, part of the Tidal Collection designed by John Whittle, Missing Link.

pages 114–15
Desk in cherry veneer, Purves and Purves; Multiplor desk organizer by Rexite with four revolving compartments, Oggetti.

pages 78–79
Glass cabinet on wheels, Purves and Purves; storage cans, from a selection, Muji; Kartell cart, The Conran Shop; medicine cabinet, SCP.

pages 122–23
Parallel shelving by Terence Woodgate, SCP; plastic lunch box, Muji; orange CD box, GTC; Ettore Sottsass glass storage jars with red, yellow, and black aniline colored beech wood caps, Oggetti.

pages 88–89
Peg board in stainless steel, Aero; Robo-stacker perforated steel drums with sandblasted toughened glass top, Jam; Parallel shelving in pressed steel designed by Terence Woodgate, SCP; Glass bowl, The Conran Shop.

pages 134–35
Garden sack and cart and galvanized bucket, from a selection, The Conran Shop.

right A bulletin board is an ideal way to keep anything from letters and receipts to bills and business cards close at hand. Pegs are screwed into baseboard, and the finished bulletin board can either be fixed to the wall with screws in each corner, hung like a painting with picture fixings, or propped against a wall.

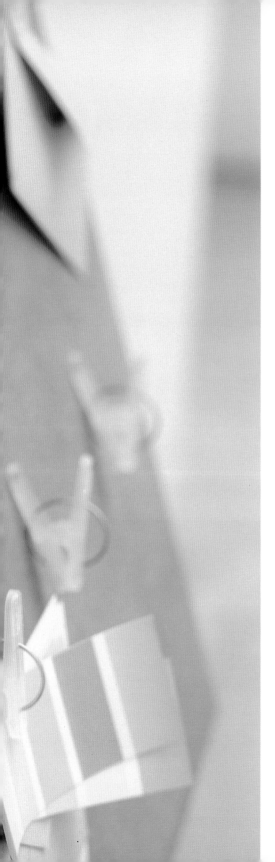

index

acknowledgments

Thank you Simon Upton for your commitment and energy throughout this project, and for capturing a sense of place and light and ease in all your photography.

Thank you everyone at Mitchell Beazley for presenting me with this opportunity and for your collective professionalism.

Thanks to Henry Bourne for kick-starting the New York trip by suggesting I contact Ellen O'Neill and Vicente Wolf. Thanks also to Debra Bourne, Miles Cockfield, Nicholas Coombe, Mats Gustafson, Charles Humphries, Neil Logan, Alfred Munkenbeck, and Stefano Tonchi for your vital support.

My biggest thanks to everyone who said yes to photography: Bob Carlos Clarke, P.J. Casey, Tricia Foley, Andrea Gentl and Marty Hyers, Janie Jackson, Markus Kiersztan and Petra Langhammer, Justin Meath Baker and Eliza Cairns, Lysander Meath Baker, Andrew Mortada, Ellen O'Neill, Gunnar Orefelt, Charles Rutherfoörd, Annabelle Selldorf, Lisa Smith and Jakob Trollbeck, Ali Tayar, Malcolm Temple, Cesar Vera,

Robert Williams, and Vicente Wolf. Thank you for welcoming us.

Thanks also to the following home owners: Ile de Re, François Gilles, Stephen & Gail Huberman, Beverley Jacomini, Jack Larson, Stephen Mack, Issey Miyake, Chris O'Connell, Chuck Rosenach, Sandra Sakarta, Seaside, The Shaker Museum, Tullie Smith House, and Stephanie Vatelot.

Thank you to all designers, retailers, press officers, manufacturers, and suppliers for loaning products for photography and for providing transparencies of products.

And finally, thank you Lawrence Morton.

Cynthia Inions

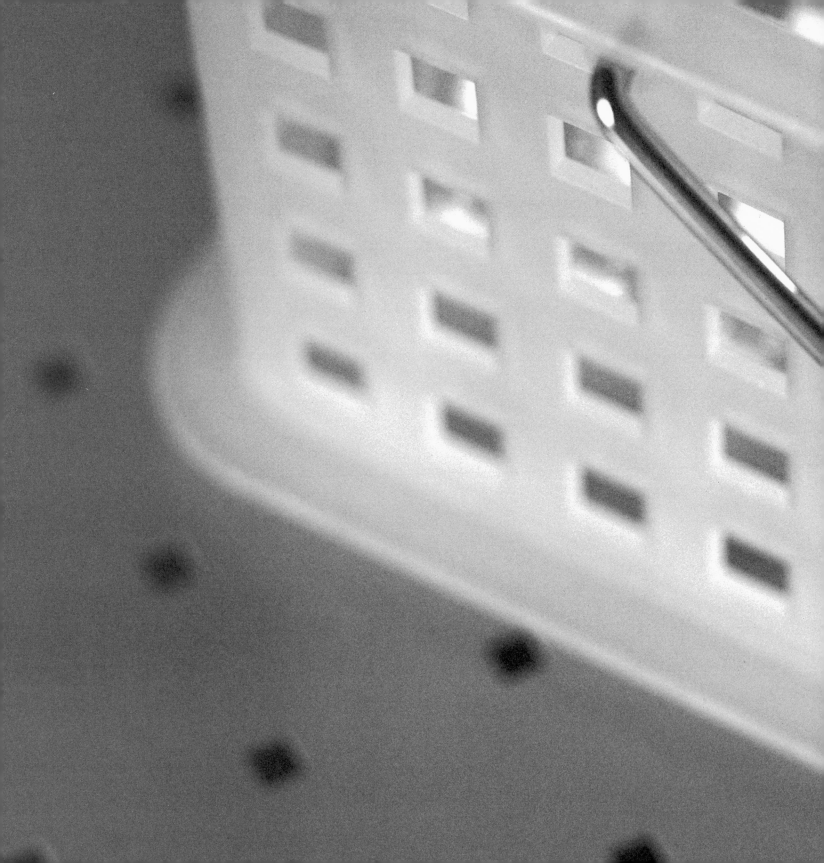